The Persian C

An autobiographical account of travel and trade in old Iran from 1903 to 1944, together with poems written in the Persian style

Leonard Flinn ('Tajir')

Edited by David Flinn and Mark Flinn

© Mark Flinn 2021

Preface

The Persian Carpet man, 'Tajir', was my father Leonard Flinn. During his long slow journeys through Iran, especially those before the days of cars and planes and international phones, he wrote frequent letters home; to his family, friends and colleagues, sometimes in excellent German or French. By keeping carbon copies of all these he dispensed with thoughts of making a journal or diary of any kind, so when he had retired in the 1950s he had this material (1000 pages or so) ready to hand, from which to compile an account of the months and years spent in his beloved Persia.

Regrettably, although a draft of a book was made it never reached publication. It is more than eighty years since the first letters were written telling about his first stay in the country, making an interesting comparison with the momentous events still prevalent in Iran today.

As the book stands, abridged and edited with the help of the original letters, it is a summary of 'Tajir's' writings. With the poems, the many anecdotes, together with a selection of his own photographs, it is hoped that it will form a worthy portrait of this Englishman abroad in the early part of the present century.

David Flinn

Corton Denham, Somerset, 1986

Foreword

As my late uncle David Flinn has pointed out in the Preface, this book is based on the accounts and letters that my grandfather, Leonard Flinn ('Tajir'), made during his five visits to Iran from 1903 to 1944. These were edited by David Flinn in the 1980s, and a typed version, illustrated by Tajir's own photographs and drawings by my late cousin Paul Flinn, was produced. My late father Michael Flinn wrote the introduction to a selection of Tajir's poems *Songs of Iran*, which follow the eight chapters of Tajir's travels.

This typed version of the travels and poems was recently bound and reprinted by my cousin Hilary Moran, and a small number of copies were sent to family members. I read this version for the first time during lockdown in early 2021 and was fascinated by the account and the accompanying photographs. I offered to republish the book, and by that process make it available through the internet to anyone with an interest in the history of Iran, Persian carpets, and the firm of Ziegler & Co.

Through a number of family meetings with Tajir in the 1960s, I developed a strong personal interest in Iran, and was motivated to travel there as a student in 1969. My route, via train to Istanbul, Black Sea steamer to Trabzon, and a series of long and dusty bus rides across arid and mountainous landscapes would have, I am sure, appealed to Tajir. On my return, I was able to report to him that the cities of Isfahan and Shiraz, and the ruins of Persepolis, remained as beautiful and evocative as they had appeared to him, sixty years earlier.

Tajir's text has been reproduced with only minor editorial changes. Place names appear as they did in his original account, with my footnotes indicating contemporary names where necessary.

Mark Flinn

Chester, 2021

IRAN

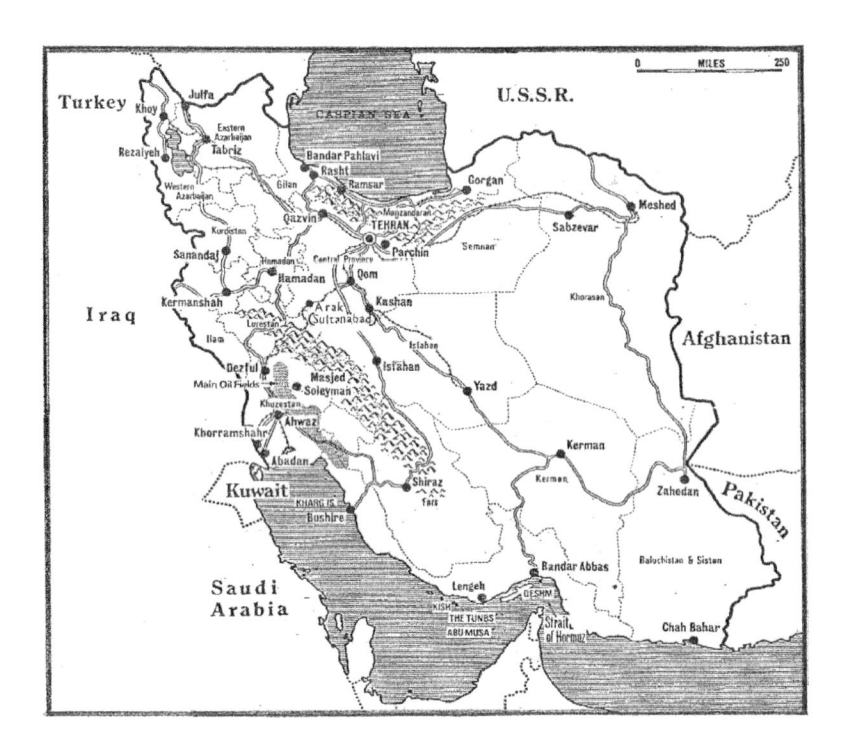

Chapter 1

Tabriz

'Whose rider in the chariot of hope has poverty for his companion'

English people when they return from a long sojourn abroad almost invariably experience a nostalgic yearning to go back again. It is easy to understand a certain desire to return to the South Sea Islands or the Isles of Greece but, curiously enough, the nostalgia seems to be stronger where the more desert places of the earth are concerned, North Africa, Syria, Iraq, Arabia or Iran radiate from a distance a glamour which was not so perceptible on the spot. It is difficult, and perhaps impossible, to define this attraction which, as an old Persian resident, affects me strongly.

There are certainly plenty of deserts in Iran, for over about two-thirds of the country, and two great stretches, are reckoned to be the worst in the world. The northerly one, the Great Salt Desert (Kavir) runs from central to eastern Iran for more than 500 miles and at its narrowest point it is about 100 miles between wells of a sort. Practically level, it is generally speaking a sea of viscous mud with here and there solid clay stretches, covered in dry weather by a thin salty crust solid enough to bear the weight of pack camels but, even for them, it is impassable in any direction in the rainy season. Within its circumference there is nothing - no vegetation, no birds, not even an insect and, in comparison with it, the Sahara has been described as a sea of blossoming meadows. To cross it was always risky, but the crossing saved about a fortnight in comparison with the safe journey round it, and camel caravans used to cross it fairly regularly in the early months of the year. With the advent of motor vehicles, time and distance shrank, even though they cannot venture into the Kavir.

Further south comes the dessicated region of south east Iran called the Dasht-I-Lut. This is somewhat smaller, and being completely waterless it has few tracks across it, and these are only usable by camels. It is impassable in summer owing to the intense heat, greater than that of Death Valley.

Sven Hedin crossed the Kavir in 1905 and two German travellers in the 1930s – Gabriel and Stratil-Sauer. The latter positively wallowed in both deserts, so evidently these terrifying places exercise some kind of fascination.

These regions are rarely visited by European travellers but the main routes used by them traverse large stretches of desolate country, which, from a traveller's point of view, are also desert. For the most part it is only a lack of water which makes them so, for wherever a water supply is practicable trees, gardens and crops flourish. In the spring too, tulips, irises, emurus and various dwarf shrubs grow over vast areas, and larkspur and other flowers flourish among the crops.

In these more travelled parts mountains are always in sight, for the most part jagged and precipitous. From Ararat, right up in the north-west curving round to Baluchistan in the south-east, there are ranges of mountains rising to 14,000 feet in places, with well-watered if narrow valleys. Ranging east from Ararat and passing south of the Caspian is the Elbours range, almost equally high, but not so complex or precipitous. Its highest peak is Demavend, 18,600 feet high forming, about fifty miles away, a conspicuous object in the Teheran scene.

For the greater part of the year the air is clear, especially about sunrise, and the atmosphere and colours baffle description. Far-off mountains seem close at hand, though a two day ride brings them apparently but a little closer. This wonderful clarity of the air, the brilliant colouring, and the sharp contrast between the desert and the sown, are things that remain in the memory long after the discomforts of travelling are forgotten. The Iranian people too are, in the main, very pleasant and easy to get on with when they are not aroused by deliberate propaganda or unreasoning fanaticism. Here again, one remembers the general tenor of one's life; and the passing annoyances of obstructive petty officials, the rather prevalent dishonesties, and the greed of buyers and sellers of most things sink, by comparison, into oblivion.

The Manchester firm of Ziegler & Co.[1] had since 1856 been established in Trebizonde on the Black Sea coast of Turkey, and then later in Iran. At first it has an office and an agent only in Tabriz, taken over from a Swiss firm Dinner, Hanhart & Co., and, as the business developed, offices were opened in other towns with European managers. At the time of its greatest development it had branches in Tabriz, Teheran, Yazd, Isfahan, Shiraz and Bushire. My father was a partner in this concern, and it was to learn the business that I was first sent to Iran, where I remained for two years. One of the first things I had to do was to learn Persian.

I am afraid that I did not study very hard in Tabriz, but I had a flair for languages, and constant contact with Iranian traders, none of whom spoke any European language, soon brought my vocabulary up to the necessary standard. Subsequent work in the many villages of the Sultanabad district was even more valuable in this connection. If, for no other reason, Ziegler & Co. deserve to be remembered for the contribution they made towards the improvement of the rug and carpet making industry in this part of the country. In the latter half of the nineteenth century this was without any form of organisation, and carpets were mostly woven in the houses of town and village dwellers, principally of the poorer class. It

---

[1] Although Ziegler's closed in 1934, their name is used to this day to describe a particular style of Persian carpet

was about 1876 that Ziegler & Co. bought a large plot of waste ground outside the town of Sultanabad[2] and on it built several dwelling houses, offices and ambars (store rooms), also a dye-house and stables, and laid out gardens. Sultanabad was then a small town of some 10,000 inhabitants and the market for a very large district devoted to the making of carpets and rugs. It controlled, as it were, the output of various types of these over a province roughly 80 miles from east to west and about the same from north to south. Within this district many types of carpets were made, differing quite visibly from each other, and from those produced in other parts of Iran.

Although of course, carpets and rugs were woven in other towns where Ziegler's had offices, the firm devoted itself in these chiefly to general commerce of which by far the most important articles were cotton and woollen piece goods, so that in my six month stay in Tabriz I became well acquainted with the Iranian trading system. But in those days Isfahan was the most important distributing centre in Iran for piece goods, so I will defer further comments about this until a later chapter.

"Please, sir, the cab's come", said the maid from the morning room door. The cab, mark you, not the taxi, for this was October 1903, long before taxis appeared on the streets of

---

[2] This town is now named Arak

Manchester. So it was in a cab that I set out for my first journey to Iran, the first of six journeys as it turned out. I picked up a travelling companion in London and we set off in the late autumn to Vienna, where we stayed a day or two. We crossed the Russian frontier at Volochisk[3], where our luggage underwent a thorough, but perfectly courteous search. Subsequently we travelled through Russia without supervision or control until we reached the Iranian frontier, where neither the Russians nor the Iranian authorities gave us more than the usual attention. So from Volochisk to Odessa, where we took ship for Batoum[4]. We had a couple of hours ashore at Sevastapol, calling subsequently at Yalta in the Crimea. At that time it was already a summer watering-place, although it is better known to the outside world as one of the more-or-less abortive meeting places of big men, conclusive though their deliberations may have seemed at the time. Until we reached the Sea of Asov the weather was still reasonably warm, but then an icy wind from the Caucasus brought the temperature down with a run, and the sea began to steam as if it was boiling. Landing at Batoum, we stayed for a night, and then went on by train for Tiflis[5] where a business friend met us and looked after us. I often wonder what the Hotel de Londres is like today; in the early days of the century it was the last

---

[3] In present-day Ukraine
[4] In present-day Georgia
[5] Tibilisi, capital of Georgia

great one of its kind for those going into the Middle East, until they reached Bombay.

The Transcaucasian railway ended at Erivan[6], a ramshackle town dominated by Mount Ararat, and it was there that our first difficulties arose. These had nothing to do with police or politics; Erivan had not had much contact with the outside world, and though we were possessed of English, French, German, Italian and Persian none of these seemed of much use in a town which ran rather to Russian, Armenian, Turkish and whatever other by-products of the Tower of Babel, which served as a means of communication in the environs of the resting place of the Ark. However, with the help of hotel staff, an Iranian and a Russian officer who only spoke Russian but was good at guessing, and aided by diagrams and figures on bits of paper we managed to charter a post carriage to Julfa on the Iranian frontier. This was an enormous landau holding six people and proved a very comfortable introduction to the posting system, identical to that which was in use in England over 100 years ago. Finally we got away only nine hours later than we originally arranged for. Our contract allowed us four post horses at every stage, the road was good and the horses were forthcoming everywhere. We drove all night and all next day till dusk when we arrived at Nakhichevan, said to be the burial place of Noah. Throughout the journey the scenery is

---

[6] Yerevan, the capital of Armenia

dominated by Mount Ararat, where according to legend the Ark grounded, and the natives firmly believe that remains of it may still be found on the summit. It consists of an isolated mountain mass, rising up into two perfectly conical craters, extinct now and covered for most of the year in snow, the higher of the two being about 16,800 feet above sea level.

Here again we had a little trouble, mostly due to the language difficulty. It appeared that our royal landau was too heavy for the bad, loose and hilly road that lay between us and Julfa, so it was finally arranged that we were to have a much smaller one, which required only two horses. By this time it was 9 pm, and the driver did not want to start until daylight, but by means of a small transfer of cash he was persuaded that midnight was the best time for anyone who wanted to go to Julfa to set out. The road was certainly bad, and the dust was awful as we kept passing long caravans of heavily laden camels.

And so, after a most uncomfortable night, we arrived at Russian[7] Julfa on the river Aras which forms the frontier with Iran. The Russian Customs formalities did not delay us unduly and we were soon on a ferry which took us across the river to the Iranian side. Here the Chief of Customs merely ordered one trunk to be opened, just glanced at the contents, and offered us a cup of tea. Ziegler & Co.'s manager in Tabriz had sent a carriage to meet us with a servant to look after us. He

---

[7] In present-day Azerbaijan

was also a good cook, and having spotted us from the river bank had prepared an enormous breakfast while we were occupied with Customs. Replete, we got into our carriage and drove off en route for the village of Marand where we stayed the night.

The road was good, laid out in such a way that it was obviously intended to serve as a permanent way for a future railway, which indeed was subsequently built. In the late afternoon we arrived at Marand where the accommodation, though primitive to my unaccustomed eyes, was by Iranian travelling standards good. Later on in fact I would have considered it almost luxurious in comparison with some of the dreadful hovels in which I had to spend the night. The room had windows, there were some rugs on the mud floor and a fireplace which did not smoke much; ample provisions and a man who knew how to cook them. A tin basin provided a cold wash, and the other place was a semi-private mud hut built over a slot in the ground. Soon after it became light we were off again, and two hours before reaching Tabriz we met friends who had driven to meet us. I wish I could have filmed the race across the level plain which ensued. Four carriages abreast were driven at breakneck speed by excited drivers who stood up and lashed their horses into the greatest speed of which their wretched animals were capable.

My first winter in Iran was a very severe one; for several consecutive nights there were 40 degrees of frost and the total snowfall amounted to several feet. In normal winters fairly heavy snowfall is general over the western half of Iran owing to the high altitude of the plateau and to the formidable ranges of mountains which appear as more or less isolated massifs in various parts. With the exception of the small towns of Kum[8] and Kashan on the fringe of the great deserts which occupy most of the eastern half of Iran, the chief centres of population lie over 5,000 feet above the sea. Teheran is about 3,800 feet up.

Early in April I was taken on an excursion from Tabriz to Bakshaish and Heris, which with a few other villages turn out a type of carpet with a very individual texture and design not found anywhere else in Iran. Generally speaking these carpets have a rather coarse and heavy cotton warp and the knots are formed of thicker woollen yarns than are generally used elsewhere. The designs too are peculiar to the district, very formal, floral, almost geometrical designs; the finest qualities make most attractive and decorative floor coverings. For me it was an arduous ride, never having been on horseback for more than two hours at a time, and the distance was about 45 miles over very rough country. However I came through pretty well and we spent the day riding around

---

[8] Now normally transliterated as Qom

several villages inspecting the progress of a few dozen carpets which were being made for us.

Spring was well on its way, the ground had dried up and it became very hot in the sun. We were able to start tennis – the courts were a layer of mud and chopped straw, a material used for the building of houses all over Iran. When skilfully laid down and rolled it makes a perfect surface.

A fortnight later I set out for Teheran, the capital. As far as Zenjan, about mid-way, the track in spring is impassable for carriages so I had to traverse this stretch on pack-horses to Zenjan and from there by fourgon[9]. By leaving a day before the post I found horses in all the chaparkhanehs or posthouses. I used four horses – one for myself, one for my servant, one for the baggage and one for the post-boy. The latter's life was hard because he was responsible for bringing the horses back to the station to which they belonged. With a late start on the first day I only rode as far as Haji Aga, a spring-time lake swarming with wild fowl and across which there is a magnificent view of Salavan Dagh, a snow-clad extinct volcano nearly 15,000 feet high. A heavy thunderstorm that evening made the track very heavy for us the next day. In many parts of Iran spring ends in thunderstorms and then there is no precipitation at all until winter sets in again. Next

---

[9] A long covered wagon used for carrying baggage

day, I travelled 13 hours and covered 65 miles, not a bad effort considering the awful state of the road.

Mianeh, where I spent the night, has always been celebrated for the number and voracity of its bugs, known as gherib gez or biters of strangers; the natives are immune but fortunately the weather was not yet warm enough to lure them from their winter quarters.

Next morning's stage involved crossing the steep and stony Kaflan Kuh pass at about 7,000 feet, and the descent to the Kizil Uzen river is precipitous. On a bare, rocky mountain on the left hand side as you go down are fragments of walls and towers, at the bottom an ancient three arch bridge in partial collapse. The ruins are called Kasr-i-Dokhtar, the bridge Pul-e-Dokhtar – the castle and bridge of the princess. There is a legend about them which I have written in verse form[10].

There were quite a number of travellers on the move so I had some difficulty about horses at a couple of stages; some petty cash disbursed in the right quarters secured preference and eventually I was at the last stage before Teheran. Soon afterwards the enormous snow-clad cone of Demavend came into view just when a carriage appeared with Ziegler's manager and his wife, who had driven out to meet me. At one o'clock we were sitting down for lunch at his house, ending

---

[10] See Page 126

the first journey in Iran which I undertook alone, apart from an Iranian servant. It was really quite an undertaking for an inexperienced youth of 22, but I had covered only some 400 miles of the 15,000 or so which eventually formed the sum total of my wanderings within the borders of Iran.

Chapter 2

Teheran

'The King may pluck an apple in his subject's garden but his courtiers will uproot the tree'

Teheran at the time of my first visit was to me a not very attractive town. True, the upper or residential part was laid out in a rectangular fashion, but, although many of the streets were well sheltered from the sun by trees, they were unmade seas of mud in the winter and terribly dusty in summer. The water supply was inadequate and impure, the climate in summer not only very hot, but stuffy and depressing. Winters were cold with plenty of snow, but spring and autumn delightfully clear and exhilarating. A few miles to the north the first range of the Elburz mountains rise steeply from the plain, towering more than 8,000 feet above the town, yet this range itself is 6,000 feet lower than Demavend

Women in street

Today, in the town at any rate, men and women wear European dress, but at the time of which I am writing all wore

the traditional Persian clothes. Life on the streets and in the bazaars was much more colourful as regards the men, for the merchants wore the long unbuttoned coat of light coloured wool, generally slate blue or light brown with turbans and a wide waist cloth, the mullahs usually had large white turbans with waist cloths of the same colour. Not so much in evidence, the women wore the all-enveloping veil, a shapeless black garment covering them from head to foot, a fold of which was drawn across the face hiding all except the eyes. In many cases even these were hidden by a strip of white net. The peasantry and poorer classes of women in the towns used cheap printed cottons instead of the black material, varied according to the means of the wearer from silk to cotton.

Goods were transported almost wholly by animals – camels, mules, horses and donkeys; the nomadic tribes even made use of cattle and sheep for this purpose. Breeding camels and other pack animals was a great, if scattered, industry. This was almost killed off by the advent of the motor car, which then deprived the countryside of a major source of income. Added to this came the appalling rise in the cost of living so that the peasant of today is no better off materially than his predecessors.

For several weeks until the weather got really hot I lived almost opposite the American missionaries' compound, going to an office in the bazaar every day. Being a considerable distance I had a contract with a carriage driver to take me there and bring me back for a little over a shilling. We had little trade there then, but being the financial centre of the country our time was fully occupied with the firm's finances. The Imperial Bank of Persia held the concession for bank notes which were not however current in the country districts; in fact notes were printed for each town separately, legally only cashable in the town of issue. Therefore there was a very large business in commercial drafts and, according to supply, there was an agio, usually quite small, but sometimes as much as 3% one way or the other.

Very often the commercial transfers did not suffice to supply the need for ready cash, and we often had to send fairly large sums of money in actual coin by post or caravan, especially to Sultanabad where notes were not current. These were almost entirely in 2 and 1 kran pieces of silver, the kran then being worth around fourpence halfpenny[11]. In size and weight these coins corresponded roughly with our florins and shillings, so the sending of a four or five thousand pounds sterling in ninepence equivalents was very considerable.

Perhaps the biggest operation of this kind was the financing of the Russo-Afghan Boundary Commission in 1885. For this, Ziegler & Co. delivered very large sums in cash to the Commission in Meshed. They had been collected in other

---

[11] About 2p in modern currency

parts of Iran six to eight hundred miles away and transported on pack animals to their destination. Each sending had to be accompanied by a member of the European staff. On one occasion a sum of several hundred pounds was urgently needed in Meshed. The money was sent on post horse from Teheran; some five hundred and sixty miles. Riding almost continuously with only short breaks for rest, the gentleman in charge delivered the cash in under six days from Teheran. A six-figure sterling amount, the firm being repaid for their outlay by our British Government in London.

My spare time was fully occupied for there was a Social Club and a Tennis Club, both good, and I bought a horse for the modest sum of ten pounds, a wiry and spirited little animal which served me well on several long journeys. In June most Europeans moved out of town to the villages on the slopes of the mountain. Gulahek, ten miles from the centre of the city, was the property of the British Legation, and here I slept in a tent in the garden of a small house belonging to the firm's manager. Five days a week I rode into town, making a day of about 11 hours from start to finish; horse and rider were usually bathed in perspiration at the end of every trip.

That July saw one of the greatest catastrophes of modern times in Iran. Asiatic cholera spread over the whole country. City life was completely disorganised, it was possible to canter through the bazaars, usually almost as packed as a football crowd. People fled to other towns and into the countryside, thereby spreading the disease and putting themselves out of reach of help. At the height of the epidemic the daily toll of deaths rose to over 1,000. The already far from sanitary water supply became polluted and served as a carrier for the disease. Few Europeans contracted it and only two, I think, died; one of them being unfortunately the lady of the house in which I was living, possibly owing to the carelessness of servants who could not be trusted to carry out the simple precautions necessary to avoid the principal sources of infection. Scarcely anyone who took the trouble to boil all drinking water and milk, and who ate no uncooked vegetables or fruit, was attacked. The epidemic ran its course in seven or eight weeks and when we returned to our town houses in September it was all over. No official death toll figures were available but it is certain that at least 20,000 of the town's population perished.

In October when I was due to go to Isfahan I contracted a chill followed by malaria and it was a few weeks before I was completely fit. A member of the bank staff going to Bushire joined forces with me and hired a post carriage, leaving my servant to bring the horse and heavy luggage on by caravan. We turned up in Isfahan with the horse in a lamentable condition and the account of his travelling expenses was extortionate, so I had to dismiss him; his home was in Isfahan so this did not worry him unduly. I should say, however, that on subsequent journeys I was very fortunate and had some good servants whose services I remember most thankfully. One was a certain Djeffer Kuli of the village of Rudberan near Sultanabad where his household wove two or three carpets a year for the firm. He was a superior type of villager and became quite devoted to me. Years after, another one, this time an Isfahani named Meshedi Bagher, travelled extensively with me. For many years he was a most capable pishkhidmat, or butler, to successive managers of the Company in Isfahan. The name Meshedi, by the way, indicates that the person bearing it has made the pilgrimage to the shrine of the Imam Reza in Meshed; that is if the word Meshedi precedes his name. If placed after the name it merely indicates that he is a native of that town. So often I had trouble with lazy and dishonest servants it gives me great pleasure to record the names of these exceptional men.

In common with many towns in Iran, Teheran, whilst of course predominately Persian in character, contained colonies of many other races in addition to the European Legations, the Bank, Telegraphs, merchants and their staffs. Indian traders, Jews, Armenians, Russians and Turkish and Arabic speaking traders from Azerbaijan and Baghdad mixed freely in the bazaars, on the whole amicably.

Street scene

The Turks have a good story about Persians, Franks, Jews and Armenians which ran somewhat as follows:

In the beginning Allah created all the peoples of the earth and being wishful that they should all be upright and honest he began to distil the virtue of honesty in a large golden bowl. When the brew was ready he called the Archangel Gabriel saying "Bring before me all those whom I have created". The first to arrive were the Turks, for they live nearer to Allah than any other peoples. They received a large ladleful of the precious drug and went away honest and upright for all time. In their turn came the Franks and the Unbelievers who received only a little measure of the drug. There was only one ladleful left in the bowl. "Allah", exclaimed the Archangel, "here come the Jews and the Persians whom I had forgotten". "Well" said Allah, scraping the bowl, "they will have to share this between them". So the Persians and the Jews went away only half as honest as the Turks, the Franks and the Unbelievers. There was then only one drop of honesty left in the bowl, and it was only then that the Armenians turned up.

Chapter 3

Isfahan

*'He who seeks wisdom is wise
but he who thinks he has acquired it is a fool'*

Summer had been hot in Teheran, for six or seven weeks the temperature indoors had risen to 90 degrees or more in the afternoons, but autumn was delightful though still very hot in the sun. By November when I left for Isfahan it was clear and cool and the nights cold. Driving by post carriage took four days; nearly all the way the road skirts the great salt desert of eastern Iran. If in passing the salt lake some 30 miles north of Kum you could turn eastwards you would have to travel several hundred miles before reaching a house. But this would be impossible, for the desert is the kind known as the Kavir, consisting mainly of mud. Camels can cross it at its narrowest part only for a few weeks in spring, after the rains have ceased and before the fierce heat of summer sets in. You get a good impression of it from the hills close to the post house of Kushki Nuserat, a tiny oasis, and from there the horizon is as limitless as the ocean itself.

Caravan in the desert

Fifteen miles on is the town of Kum which holds the great shrine and mosque of Fatima, the sister of Imam Reza of Meshed. Partially surrounded by a great cemetery, to be buried in that holy ground constitutes a valuable visa to the passport of every true believer into the hereafter. In the mosque itself is the tomb of the great Shah Abbas, a contemporary of Queen Elizabeth I. The burnished golden dome of the mosque and its graceful minarets catch the eye from many miles away. A fanatical town this, and it would be unwise to approach too near to the mosque.

The next stop was Kashan, home of some of the finest rugs and carpets. According to the inscription woven into it, a Kashani was responsible for the weaving of the great Ardabil carpet now in the Victoria and Albert Museum. This carpet, with two similar ones, for several hundred years had been in the mosque at Arbadil, between Tabriz and the Caspian. In the early 1880s it was bought jointly by the firms of Castelli and Ziegler and brought to England. At the time it was in as many as twelve pieces, so it was carefully restored, portions of two other similar carpets being used in the process. Afterwards it was sold, passing through many hands until the Museum finally acquired it for about £2,000. Kashan was the home of the silk weaving industry for, in addition to rugs, a good deal of velvet was made there.

We went by the carriage road to Murchekar, a large well-watered village with a place in Persian history. Here it was that Nadir Kuli, who afterwards invaded India, captured Delhi and brought the Peacock Throne to Persia, and defeated an Afghan army in 1729; this being the decisive battle that put an end to the Afghan domination of the country. Here too was the district of Joshegan, famous for its finely woven carpets, but which are no longer extensively produced. Driving through the last night we arrived in Isfahan in time for breakfast, the end of my lazy carriage journeys for nearly a year, which was a good thing because one learns little about the country when one's preoccupation is to get the journey over as soon as possible. Subsequently I travelled 'caravan', riding 20-25 miles a day with pack animals, not always choosing the direct route and staying the night in villages where Europeans were rarely seen.

I have not visited Meshed or Kerman, but of all the places in Iran the one town in which I would choose to live is Isfahan. Having a better climate than Teheran it is not so oppressive in summer and less cold in winter when also less snow falls. The water supply is better, less liable to pollution, and nearly every house has a well of its own. Hence the mortality rate from cholera was on a very much lower scale here than in Teheran. It is also much older, having for some centuries been the former capital and it contains many mosques and buildings of the fifteenth to seventeenth centuries. Its origin is obscure, but this well-watered plain must always have been under cultivation. The waters of the river Zendah Rud are drawn off by many irrigation channels; under the Safavid kings, its most flourishing period, Isfahan is said to have had one million inhabitants. Certainly the vast extent of ruins east of the city is evidence of far more people than at the present time.

Jameh mosque, Isfahan

Madrasah Chahar Bagh, Isfahan

For our firm it was the main distribution centre, mainly for cotton and woollen piece goods. In a country not particularly famous for its probity in business the Isfahani merchants were certainly the best of their kind. Many carried on businesses handed down from father to son, most had made their pilgrimage to Mecca as shown by their names – Haji Mirza Mahmoud, Haji Seyed Hassan, Haji Assudullah Sempsar and many others. Being myself the son of one of our partners I had to call on them; one of them arranged to invite the leading merchants to his warehouse in one of the large caravanserais where I was duly introduced to them, and in return they were all invited to a great tea-party in the office.

The Manager's house was at the south end of the town on the great Charbargh avenue where it crosses the bridge of Allah Vezdi Khan, the longest of five bridges in the Isfahan district, each of them differing radically from the other four. As usual the house was built around a central courtyard with a water tank in the centre, a wide-roofed verandah separating the rooms from the courtyard. There was only one storey and a flat roof from which a wide view took in a long stretch of river and the jagged, precipitous peaks of the mountains beyond.

Occasional visits had to be made to some of the outstanding personalities of the town. At this time the Governor of the province was Zil-e-Sultan, a brother of the Shah and eldest son of Nasr-e-din Shah. His mother not being of royal blood, he was passed over in the succession in favour of the more highly born Muzzafer-e-din. At the death of Nasr-e-din in 1896 it is said that Zil contemplated seizing the throne, for he was then governor of Arak, Isfahan, Fars and other provinces, the most powerful man in the country. He hesitated for some days, and meanwhile the Valiadh (crown prince) dashed from Tabriz to Teheran and was proclaimed Shah. The Zil was shorn of some of his power but remained Governor of Isfahan until his death. Always favourably inclined to the English community he was most affable on the several occasions on which we visited him. In those parts of the country under his control the roads were usually safe; with his strong personality he was more feared than admired by the Iranians, especially the country tribesmen for whom robbing caravans was a normal activity. Generally speaking he ruled the province with a fair and just hand, not however without a streak of cruelty and treachery.

One personality whose influence extended far beyond the boundaries of Isfahan was the Aga Nejeffi, then one of the spiritual heads of Islam in Iran. There were never more than three or four of these chief clergy in Iran and their position might be compared to that of a medieval archbishop, possessing in addition to their supreme religious authority an almost equally great influence in matters temporal. The bulk of Mohammedan clergy were the mullahs who were preachers, teachers, schoolmasters, even judges; above them were the lords spiritual who were called mujtahids. Merit, and no doubt some influence, gained them their high office and many years study at Nejef, near Kerbala in the neighbourhood of Baghdad; coupled with an irreproachable life and meticulous adherence to the laws of Islam, these were the prime qualifications. They received no payment from, and held no office under, the government; the attainment of the rank of mujtahid seems to have been by tacit acceptance rather than by election. Their authority is second only to that of the Shah and sometimes in a clash of wills the Shah has to give way. For example, on various occasions and for no apparent reason, but probably from sheer fanaticism and desire to assert authority they would issue an edict that all European goods were 'haram', unclean, and everybody was debarred from dealing in them. At one period this occurred so frequently that our firm had a whole page in our private telegraph code devoted to this aspect of the business. The veto naturally suited nobody except the fanatics and was usually called off after a few weeks. Doubtless it cost the merchants something in the form of pious offerings.

Other interruptions to the normal flow of business were robberies on the roads and disputes with the Customs authorities. Not that business was ever as easy or as smooth as in England. Once I took ten days to buy a rug. The price asked was 180 tomans. My first offer was 95, and the bargain was eventually struck at 120 plus a 'present' of 5 tomans. The clerical staffs of the Bank, Indo-European Telegraph Dept., and the European concerns were made up chiefly of Armenians who were normally proficient in both Persian and English, the rest of the staff being Iranians. This was a good system, both groups were jealous of each other and watched each other like hawks. The Armenians lived in the large suburb of Julfa outside town. Originally they had been brought to Isfahan by Shah Abbas about the year 1590 when he moved his court from Kasvin. During his campaign in the North West he had seen for himself that Armenians were superior in skill to Persians in all sorts of arts and crafts. He therefore ordered the inhabitants of Julfa, a sizeable town on the present Russian border, to remove to Isfahan in order to utilise them rebuilding his city[12]. He gave them land to build themselves a town, allowed them to practice their own Christian religion, build churches and schools and they rapidly became a flourishing community. It is said 160,000 people were involved in the transfer but this is certainly a gross exaggeration. Badly treated by the successors of Shah Abbas, towards the end of the nineteenth century the population of Julfa had shrunk to a few thousand. Under the more enlightened and tolerant Zil-e-Sultan they were given back most of their privileges and rapidly gained prosperity.

---

[12] This is a highly sanitised version. For a more accurate account see https://en.wikipedia.org/wiki/Julfa,_Azerbaijan_(city)

Isfahan at the time of my first visit was by far the biggest distribution centre in Iran. Not only did it lie nearly in the geographical centre of the country, but the main caravan route from the Gulf to the Caspian passed through it while other roads branched off east and west. Many of the Teheran merchants relied for their supplies of textiles and other imported goods on the merchants of the Isfahan bazaars, while Isfahan copper and silverware was sold all over Iran. Kalemkars (literally penwork) or curtains, hand painted by means of wood blocks, on imported white shirtings, found a ready sale to almost every town and country house, and ever since I have had a house of my own I have used them and sent a few pairs over quite recently.

One of the most important exports of Iran has always been opium. It is the raw material of morphia, codeine and other medical drugs so the demand for it is considerable but this can easily be satisfied by a small proportion of the quantity grown in various countries such as Asia Minor and Bulgaria, in addition to Iran and India. It was to satisfy the demand of the opium smoker (and eater) that caused vast areas of arable land to be given over to poppy cultivation. Since World War I great efforts have been made to reduce the production of opium for non-medical purposes through a special department of the League of Nations. To this end an International Opium Convention was drawn up with the object of curtailing its production, but Iran, though approving it, did not sign it.

Poppy fields

Opium was one of the many things which became monopolies of the government, but for opium the monopoly only extended to the handling and disposal of the crop, not to the growing of it. The government would announce from time to time that the area under poppy cultivation was being reduced in favour of wheat growing, but one wonders to what extent this was really the case. Just around the outbreak of war in 1939 several hundred cases of Iranian opium were imported into Britain and duly taken up by the big manufacturing chemists under Home Office licence. Control was so rigid that they had to be accounted for to the Customs to three decimal places of an ounce!

Work in the office went on steadily until a few days before Noruz, Iran's New Year's Day, March 21st. Invariably at this time of year little trading took place; the ending of the holiday was 'Sizdahyum', the thirteenth day after Noruz when it was the custom to go out into the gardens and fields for a picnic. By now I had gained a good working knowledge of trading methods and it was time to move on again, this time to Sultanabad where conditions were totally different, for the activities of the firm there consisted solely in the production and buying of carpets and rugs. So far I had travelled as quickly as possible from point to point. Except in the course of ordinary business transactions I had not really come into close contact with Iranian people, but now I had the chance to get off the beaten track to travel around among the villagers and peasants who form the vast bulk of the population. Although I had not then read the work, if indeed it was already in existence, I put to practical use the sentiment expressed by Flecker in *Hassan*: -"We travel not for trafficking alone".

> *"Sweet to ride forth at evening from the wells,*
> *When shadows pass gigantic on the sand,*
> *And swiftly through the silence beat the bells*
> *Along the golden road to Samarkand.*
> *We travel not for trafficking alone,*
> *By hotter winds our fiery hearts are fanned,*
> *For lust of knowing what should not be known*

We take the golden road to Samarkand".

For the Iranians, time was not so valuable; "Fard-inshallah"- tomorrow if it please Allah – was certainly not without its influence. You knew that a certain journey, on horseback of course, would take a minimum of seven days, it mattered therefore little if by wandering somewhat off the direct route it took eight or nine. Many years later when motoring was general and nobody rode anywhere, this habit of straying off the beaten track came in very useful as will be seen in due course.

Chapter 4

Sultanabad and the West

'It is not age that brings wisdom but experience'

So in April 1904 I hired a muleteer and three mules to convey me to Sultanabad, using my own horse 'Flypaper' for myself. Early on the 8th I rode out from Isfahan, at first nearly an hour through narrow streets and then through fields to an old caravanserai where I halted for lunch. Ain-i-Shirvan was the last building for many miles; I rode for three hours through a stony desert to Chal-e-Siah, a small oasis with a few struggling fruit trees and a meagre water supply. The inhabitants lived in abject poverty and I had to stay the night in a very dirty room so that it was lucky that insect life was still dormant. Tea and some eggs were forthcoming, though, and I had my camp bed and my own provisions.

Village market scene

Next day I was sitting outside another ruined caravanserai to eat my lunch. As soon as the muleteer arrived he urged me to move off at once. Very bad people here, he said, and they would probably rob me. Several men had come out of the village nearby and gone away without speaking; if they were friendly they usually hung around asking lots of questions. So off we went, reaching the village called Dehak in a couple of hours, picturesquely located at the foot of rocky mountains, still snow-covered. The largest village on my route was Khomein lying on a little river, where I had an excellent room with a large portrait of Kaiser Wilhelm II for company. From here on there were several villages where our carpet weavers lived, particularly at Gili, the water of which had some virtue imparting a special sheen to dyed red wool. From here it was only 15 miles to Sultanabad and halfway I was met by three members of the staff with several servants, arriving at the Kaleh (walled compound) Ziegler at midday.

Most towns in Iran can boast of a reasonable antiquity, not so Sultanabad. Up to the end of the eighteenth century the chief place of this district was Moshgabad, the name of which survives in a certain type of carpet. The inhabitants had taken to wholesale robbery to such an extent that the Shah of the day ordered them to be driven out and the town razed to the ground. It was never rebuilt. The new town, Sultanabad, at first called Shehr-e-No (New Town) was erected 25 miles away under the northern edge of the mountains where the alluvial plain slopes down to the salt lake. Although there are no permanent streams in the plain, there is plenty of subsoil water near the mountains; scores of villages in the plain are dependent on a kanat or underground aqueduct, sometimes several miles long, the surplus water of which flows into the salt lake.

Ziegler's manager, Theodor Strauss, was due to start shortly on a visit to Hamadan, Senneh and Kermanshah to buy wool for the manufacture of carpets, and I was due to accompany him. We were going into dangerous country and would probably fare better in some places by camping rather than relying on village accommodation. The firm's establishment lay at a little distance to the south of the town, just at the entrance to the valley of a small river called the Kera Rud. Here we assembled quite a cavalcade: eight mules carrying all our impediments, tents and so on, seven mounted and armed servants, two carriages, one belonging to an American missionary doctor and his wife, and the other a very large vehicle conveying the Strauss family.

The mule cavalcade

There was no road for carriages except in the plain where it was possible for them to do two stages to the caravan's one. Accordingly I left the day before they did, and barring a severe thunderstorm miles from anywhere, had no trouble in reaching Sarukh in the afternoon, some 25 miles from Sultanabad.

The village of Sarukh has given its name to a fine make of rug originally woven here and in neighbouring villages, but if all the rugs and carpets subsequently christened Sarukhs had been woven here it would have had about 20,000 people instead of about 800. The carriage party overtook us the next day at Dizabad when a friend arrived from Hamadan to meet us. After Nishehr the road was stony and undulating with several miles of fields and gardens before we arrived at Hamadan. Many years after this journey, it is interesting to read an account by M. de Thevenot of his ride from Hamadan to Isfahan in 1664. The description reads as if it had happened simultaneously with my own, so little had conditions changed during the 240 years which separated us. His book *Travels into the Levant* was published in London in 1687.

Ruins in Hamadan

Hamadan, the ancient Ecbatana, capital of the empire of the Medes, lies over 6,000 feet above sea level. Of the Median splendour nothing remains except fragments of columns and old walls built into the present houses; also the Musallah, a long mound which may have been the site of the treasure house of Cyrus, at one end of which there was a battered old stone lion. In summer, nights are cool though winter is severe and the many-founted Elwend, the *Mons Orontes* of the ancients, provides an excellent water supply even in the driest of seasons. Water, or the lack of it, is one of the biggest headaches of Iran's internal economy.

Village scene

Unencumbered by missionaries, women or children, two days after arriving in Hamadan, Strauss and I set out for Senneh at the head of our seven riders and eight mules. The first night we were without bedding as the mule carrying it had shaken his load off into the river. Things were almost at famine prices for, due to the bad harvest of the previous year, there was little bread to be bought for ourselves and no barley for the animals. So landowners were sitting on their own stocks to their very great profit. Conditions were said to be even worse towards Senneh so we decided to cut out that part of our trip and make for Kermanshah via the Kurdish town of Sungur. Several of the men said that they knew the way but were afraid to go for it was a lawless country. Eventually, by offering a very large enam or present of money we secured the services of a guide. It is true he set us on the right path but after seven or eight miles he proved quite useless so we dispensed with him. It was a difficult day's ride; by ten o'clock we were going over snowfields up to a pass at nearly 10,000 feet. Most of the ascent and descent were through narrow glens not unlike the highlands of Scotland where there were many types of game birds, pigeons, sand-grouse and snipe. After nearly fourteen hours and forty miles we rode into Sungur.

This is a purely Kurdish town, and the inhabitants resented our coming. Traditional Iranian hospitality was conspicuous by its absence so it was only after some delay we found shelter in a small caravanserai. About midnight a man more friendly than the rest told us quietly that a great discussion was going on as to the best means of robbing us, because of course we were well armed. Having no wish to start an international incident, like the Arabs we folded our tents and silently stole away an hour before dawn. During the morning we stopped for tea at a lovely tea house or chai khaneh. There were seven or eight men there and when we came to mount again we discovered we were a rifle short. All questioning failed to discover the missing weapon, so we threatened to beat up those present starting with the owner. He said he would get a much venerated old seyid from nearby to come with a Koran and make everybody swear thereon that they had not taken the rifle. One man refused to take the oath, went out and brought in the rifle. When he had seen it stacked against the wall he had got onto the flat roof, lain down and noiselessly reached over and taken it up. Hiding it in a wheatfield he quietly rejoined the company at the tea house. Clever, but not quite clever enough, for he would probably never hear the last of it for a long time from the owner, for we omitted to pay for the tea after thanking the seyid for his help.

A little way up the side valley lies Bernatch, the home village of several semi-nomadic families. The local bread was composed chiefly of acorns, there was no grain for the horses but grazing seemed very good so we stayed for two nights as we all needed a rest. Then, going up the valley towards a pass called Tang-e Sizdah-Kharan (valley of the thirteen thorns), at the top we found an encampment of Kurd nomads who presented bowls of buttermilk; very refreshing, for the weather had turned warm and the last of the rains were behind us. I had no more until November.

On reaching Kermanshah our agents reported the wool which had been bought on our behalf was now in the process of being washed in the river, and the transactions would not be completed for another ten days or so. The attractions of Kermanshah are soon exhausted, the chief ones being the views of the town from some distance off and the peak of Kuh-e-Parrao some 12,000 feet high. The local manager of the Imperial Bank with whom we were staying had several friends amongst the Kurdish petty chieftains, and one of them, hearing that we had time at our disposal, offered to take us around the district to introduce us to some of his neighbours. On the third day therefore we went with our entire cavalcade north out of town twelve miles to Sarab-e-Nilifur, pitching tents in the garden of our host. The same happened the following day; each evening an enormous meal was provided, set out on the floor, all to be eaten with the fingers of course. Our host spotted a bottle of whisky amongst our belongings, asked what it was and on being told that it was medicine said we must bring it it along to supper, at which meal he consumed fully two-thirds of it without any apparent effect. Our last bottle too, but if you are used to the local arak, which is about 100% alcohol, I suppose whisky is just mildly soothing.

Next day at Rowanser we took leave of our Kurdish friends to traverse a difficult path in limestone country. Being hot and thirsty work without surface water, I slaked my thirst by chewing the stem of wild rhubarb, growing plentifully here. Back again at Kermanshah it took two more days to settle our wool account and return to Hamadan. One afternoon on the way, by wearing tennis shoes I managed to climb up to the great rock carving and trilingual translations of Darius, a climb rarely done without artificial aid although some locals manage it with bare feet.

Part of this ride was truly delightful through English-seeming lanes with masses of roses and other wild flowers to the town called Kengaver. Later, passing a freshwater swamp we secured some duck and snipe for the larder, deciding to stay a couple of days at the nearby village of Tuisirkan, a picturesque place where many roofs and verandahs are made of wood instead of the usual mud and straw plaster.

Two days were spent on business back at Hamadan, on the third we rode out again up the Abbassabad valley to see the rock inscription of Xerxes: like that of Darius it too is trilingual and in cuneiform. Iranians call it Ganj Nameh, the Tale of the Treasure, saying that anyone who can read it will find the treasure buried nearby. Also we climbed a local peak, a place of pilgrimage on the summit of which there is a ruined stone structure supposedly the grave of Seth, the son of Adam!

Four days later we were back in Sultanabad after a most interesting journey of 600 miles with a good deal of hard physical work in it. I lost several pounds in weight and it toughened me considerably so that I was able to ride all day if necessary, even in the height of summer. My flesh was the colour of my saddle and besides I was in very good health. Not so the horses, only four out of nine were really fit for work on our return. No wonder, when at one period of our tour we were 61 hours on the road in six days.

The carpet industry was wholly a village or cottage occupation, all carpets and rugs being worn in the weavers' houses. About 1876, Ziegler & Co. had decided to go to Sultanabad and develop the carpet trade there on a sound basis. There were about 40 looms then in the town itself but all carpets and rugs from surrounding districts came to its market. The Company's premises, known as Fort Ziegler because of its enclosing 16 foot wall, contained offices, storerooms, dye-houses, dwellings and gardens. The dye-houses were the most important for they ensured the use of fast and properly harmonised colours. Most of the carpets were woven independently and contained aniline-dyed wool; these colours were not only glaring but soon faded. Much of the weaving too had degenerated, being coarse and uneven.

Within ten years there were about twelve hundred looms in the town and other European firms began to appear. Demand for these much-improved carpets grew as did the competition for the services of the weavers in the town. Village weavers became more and more eager to work for the European companies and so Ziegler's gradually came to have more carpets in work there than in Sultanabad itself.

Fort Ziegler and photographer

In 1893 the British Council in Isfahan reported: *'In no town of Persia have I seen such evidence, not of wealth quite, but of well-doing and well-being. Here people are comfortably dressed and look confident and happy, they all live on the carpet weaving - its good effects are evident in the whole community. ……..no place impressed me so much as Sultanabad'.*

To maintain a steady turnover it was necessary to have several hundred looms going at any one time and dozens of them featured in our production chart. The village looms were as much as forty miles from town and constant inspection was necessary to ensure that the carpets were being duly woven. To get the colourings and designs we wanted we provided the weaver with a weaving pattern called wagireh, together with the necessary amount of dyed wool for the various colours.

Carpet weaving

At first, locally current types of designs were used drawn by Persian designers employed by the firm, from which the weaving patterns were made. Later other designs were introduced based on Persian carpets illustrated in works of art or copied from other rugs and carpets. Our biggest design undertaking was creating a copy of the great Ardabil carpet; an extremely expensive affair made to the order of an American customer.

Weaving prices were fixed per square yard, to use an English measurement, and a cash advance given when the weaver took the dyed wool away; then the carpet would be woven by the women and girls. A local agent, very often a weaver himself, was supposed to watch over our interests but one was up against the fact that the average peasant was neither very honest nor very diligent, hence the need for constant supervision. A very curious relationship developed between the individual weavers and ourselves whereby we became both policemen and judges in our own cause. It seems contrary to justice and fair dealing that a creditor should take the law into his own hands, maintained very often by a show of force; but both sides preferred the system to intervention by the governor and his mamurs (a kind of policeman) who were invariably corrupt, veritable bloodsuckers in fact.

In one case, a village where we had a number of weavers was robbed of many of its sheep by men from another village with whom they had a feud. We had no carpets in the village of the aggressors and many of our weavers had been rendered destitute. So one fine day we appeared at the pasturage with eight sowars (armed riders) and drove off 400 sheep the 15 miles to Sultanabad. The contending parties then had the choice of having the whole dispute, including the sheep, handed over to the authorities, or to accept our arbitration. As a result we managed to terminate the feud and everyone got all their sheep back (or nearly all!).

It must not be thought that our display of armed force on those expeditions was merely to overawe recalcitrant weavers, it was also very desirable for self-protection. Once when I was going round the Kemereh district some gazelles crossed the track in front of us. Immediately there was a 'view haloo' together with much futile firing from horseback. Breasting a small rise in the ground there appeared a village half a mile away; the villagers, hearing the shooting, all turned out and started to fire on us. We rushed them and were received with abject apologies. We were thought to be robbers who had looted an adjoining village the previous day; meanwhile the men who had shot at us took sanctuary in the mosque. We confiscated their arms. I once took back with me five defaulting weavers, some of their carpets for other dealers, a couple of donkeys and a few odd cooking pots. It was gratifying to find that these people rarely bore malice, in fact many of them would turn up in quite a short time asking for further contracts, only grinning when reminded of their former delinquencies.

Chapter 5

To the Gulf

*'There are many treasures in the sea,
but safety lies on the shore'*

It was pleasant to live for a few weeks in a large European circle. In Sultanabad there were only five Europeans, whereas in Isfahan, in addition to Ziegler's people, there were the staffs of the Imperial Bank, the Indo-European Telegraphs, Church Missionary Society and the British Consulate-General. I had now obtained a good working knowledge of the various activities of our concern and could also speak what I might call basic Persian fairly fluently. There were still two places to visit before returning home: Shiraz and Bushire, a journey of about 600 miles by the most direct route.

So I got together a little caravan and bought a yabu from a muleteer for myself. A yabu is a packhorse, and the name is used as a term of contempt much as we might apply the word mongrel to a dog. It was not a prepossessing animal but it carried me well enough; when I sold it in Bushire I only lost £1, not a high price to pay for transporting myself that distance. I dispatched my little caravan consisting of my servant, a muleteer and four mules, and a few hours later rode out after them across the great bridge. The ground rose steadily over the stony, alluvial slopes coming from the Kuh-e-Sufa. A little spring by the roadside is called the Chesmeh-e-Khoda Hafiz, the spring of goodbye, for it is at that point that is was the custom of the Iranians to accompany departing travellers; hereabouts is the last view of Isfahan.

There is nothing striking in the next few stages except at Surnek where there is a shapeless ruin, scarcely more than a mud heap, said to be the remains of the hunting lodge of Bahram V, a fifth century king of the Sassanian dynasty. This king was passionately devoted to the chase, especially of the wild ass, an extremely swift-footed animal, hence his soubriquet of Gur, the wild ass. According to legend Bahram met his death hunting this creature by plunging into a swamp somewhere to the south of Kushk-e-zard. Hearing this legend inspired me to write verses[13] during the many leisure hours of the journey; a day's trek is rarely more than six hours with a caravan and one cannot all the time be hobnobbing with the local peasantry and muleteers in the tea-house.

Quite close to the track near Pasagardae is the tomb of Cyrus amid ruins of which only the foundations remain; there being no one about I had the chance to examine it thoroughly. Beyond this plain we came to the valley of the Polvar, the most attractive scenery of the whole route, full of trees and

---

[13] See 'Bahram Gur', Page 111

flowers backed by high hills where the decisive battle between the Medes and the Persians is said to have been fought. Woodpigeons, dove, partridge and chough as well as the ubiquitous blue rock pigeon abound, so there is good sport; herons and kingfishers too.

High on a cliff above the river is the tomb of Darius and the Sassanian sculptures of Shapur; legend has it that King Shapur represents the national mythological hero Rustem. Passing round a low spur I came upon the ruins of Persepolis and found myself in a dilemma. I am no archaeologist, and any description I might venture on the historic spot would probably be a re-hash of the writings of experts. Yet simply to set down that I went to Persepolis, had a look round and then rode away would be apt to give the impression that the great names of history mean but little to me; on the contrary I am intensely interested. An ignorant merchant from Manchester, as an Iranian newspaper once called me (on the principle of course that if you have a bad case you should abuse the other fellow) cannot add anything to the sum total acquired and made known by archeologists and historians. We can do little more than absorb some of this knowledge; seeing that a certain Bishop Stuart arrived in a carriage a few minutes after I did is precisely what happened, for he was an authority on Iran and we spent several hours together.

Views of the ruins and reliefs at Persepolis

Next morning I crossed the Polvar, which hereabouts becomes the Bendemeer. Poetic licence is carried pretty far by Moore[14], when he sings of bowers of roses and nightingales by Bendemeer's stream. I allow myself a little bias in that direction sometimes, but I suppose the greater the poet, the greater the licence for there are no roses anywhere near the Bendemeer and if possible fewer nightingales. On the fifteenth day out of Isfahan suddenly the road dips sharply to the right and there, framed by two rocky hills lies the town of Shiraz, with its domes, cypress trees and gardens. The pass is called the Teng-e-Allah Akbar, God is great, the traveller exclaims when he sees his goal lying invitingly before him.

I spent a fortnight in Shiraz; the weather being perfect, fairly hot in the sun and very cool at night. There is an exceptionally fine brick-built bazaar here, said to be the finest in the Middle East. The gardens are unique in Iran, being laid out in terrace form on the slopes from the hills. Here also are the graves of two of the greatest Persian poets, Hafiz and Sadi, though they wore a very neglected look. In addition to the resting places of famous poets, the roses, nightingales and so forth, Shiraz is known throughout Iran for its repoussé silverwork, mosaic frames and boxes, of which I bought some specimens; also its wine, some bottles of which cheered me on the way to

---

[14] Thomas Moore, Irish poet (1779-1852)

Bushire. It is the colour of Malaga but heavier and more potent.

After dinner one evening early in November I left the town, having previously despatched my caravan to await me at a caravanserai eight miles along the route. It is an eerie feeling to ride alone on an unknown track on a dark night. Moonless, the sky seemed full of stars; there was not a sound to be heard save that of the horses' hooves on the stony way. A Russian merchant going to Bushire also joined me a couple of days on the way and together we rode up the pass of the old woman, the Kotal-e Pir-e Zan. Passing through a forest of small oak trees we reached the summit, 7,400 feet above sea level, just as the sun broke through a few minutes before setting, and I did not have rain again until I got back to England.

The Russian gentleman stumbled along after me, groaning and cursing the whole time. He may have been a good businessman, but he was certainly a bad traveller. The yard of the caravanserai was crowded with mules through which we had to push our way. Following a good meal I could sleep very little owing to the hideous noise of bells of the several hundred mules assembled in the courtyard, and the attention of a variety of insects. These had a congenial breeding place in an enormous manure heap, which probably went back further in time that the caravanserai itself.

Three days later, having lost the Russian while shooting game for my larder, we crossed a small rocky plateau from where one saw an immense plain studded with palm trees. Leaving about midnight before our last trek I was so sleepy I had to dismount repeatedly to avoid finding myself on my back in the desert. Soon, after a gorgeous sunrise, Bushire appeared in the distance, looking like one of Turner's pictures of Venice. We came out on the shore of the lagoon at Shief, a sailing boat awaiting to take me across to Bushire. This was the first time I had seen the sea for two years and I enjoyed the seven mile sail. It had taken five and a half days to ride 170 miles over one of the worst roads in the world; how I wondered had that old man, the bishop, stuck it out at his advanced age. I believe he was about 80 at the time and had undertaken the long journey from Isfahan to be in New Zealand for Christmas.

Sunset over the Gulf

The conditions of work and travel so far described remained very much the same until the outbreak of war in 1914 and generally speaking the internal condition of the country deteriorated. Owing to the weakness of the central government there was little control over the activities of the nomad tribes; communications between the Gulf and the interior were often interrupted by their forays. Just at that time, however, things were fairly quiet in the south so I had no trouble on my journey. It was November when I arrived, and the residents said the 'cool' weather had begun. To me who had come from the bracing uplands it seemed intolerably hot and stuffy. I weighed myself before I left Bushire and found I had lost a stone in weight since setting out from England, although I apparently had no reserve of embonpoint to lose. Nevertheless, I was in perfect condition and played tennis the evening on the day on my arrival there.

At the British Residency at Sabzabad I was fortunate to meet Sir Percy ('the Major') Cox. I met him again years later when he was President of the Royal Geographical Society after his retirement when we had several long talks about Iran.

So at last after two years in the country I went on board a British India mail steamer, transferring to the P. & O. at Bombay. Thence overland from Marseilles to London and Manchester, home in time for Christmas 1905.

Chapter 6

Two Journeys 1907-1909

'Confession is the best excuse'

After I had been home for a few months, the daily round seemed to be humdrum after the experiences of the past two years, but travelling was over for the time being; I just had to stifle my wanderlust and get on with the trafficking. Before I went to Iran the only book I had read about the country was Curzon's *Persia* and I think I skipped a good deal of this. Now I read it with possessive interest, I sought out books at second-hand shops, so that at the time of writing I have collected over a hundred volumes, from Marco Polo to the present day[15]. Iran in fact became my hobby as well as my business interest, so that as time went on I added book-lore to the practical experience gained in successive journeys.

As things turned out it was nearly two years before I was sent again, and in the interval the internal state of Iran became one of increasing unrest. In 1906 there was a revolution and the Shah was forced to grant a constitution, which included setting up a Majless or Parliament. The authority of the

---

[15] This collection, along with Tajir's collection of Persian coins, was donated to the Iran Society of London on his death, and is deposited in the library of Wadham College, Oxford.

Majless waxed and waned until the abdication of Reza Shah in 1941, but it is now in effective control of the country's affairs.

The years 1906 and 1907 saw a considerable extension of the Company's business and in October of the latter year I went off once more taking with me two new recruits for the staff in Iran. I followed the same route as before via Vienna, Odessa, Batoum and Tiflis. The railway had been pushed forward as far as the frontier, with a bridge over the river Araxes. Snow and bitter winds prevailed all the way from Julfa to Tabriz and of course travel in Iran was on the same old lines, even though a railway was poking its nose over the frontier. I did not stay long in Tabriz, the two young men had no experience of riding so we had to take two carriages, each driven by four horses. Travelling in this way we could do only one or at most two stages a day, so it took us a fortnight to reach Teheran. No fewer than nine times we crossed streams, having to use the river bed. At each passage water washed over the floor of the carriages, little open dorushkas with hoods that had to be firmly lashed to keep them open. At Zendjan both road and weather improved; we were told that there had been a riot and the Governor had been chased out of town by an irate population, though I had forgotten what the quarrel was about. This was a slow and rather boring journey which compared unfavourably with the previous trip by horse and post carriage of five and a half days. Truly he who travels fastest who travels alone. Two days were sufficient for me in Teheran before going on to Sultanabad.

Crossing a bridge

Before Christmas I went for a few days to inspect certain villages in the Mahallat region. Conditions were very difficult for us because weavers, like everybody else, had been affected by the general atmosphere of unrest and lawlessness all over the country. A fortnight after I got back we received an S.O.S. from our agent in the Kemareh district. A certain local provider (he would have been a robber baron on a small scale in Europe in the Middle Ages) had been terrorising and robbing villages with a band of forty horsemen. The people of Rudberan all fled when they heard that he was in the neighbourhood, our agent sending a message to say if we wanted him we would find him in the mountain behind the village. I went out with seven armed servants to investigate. The inhabitants were all coming back nearly as fast as they had run away, the local bandit having returned to his own village without molesting them, so I thought the best thing to do was to pay him a visit. He was affability itself and had avoided raiding villages in which we were interested to any great extent. On parting, he presented me with a gold coin which I hope was his own property.

At another village, Sheveh, I found that the agent had become a complete rogue, on one pretext or another had taken our dyed wool away from the weavers with which he wove carpets for Iranian dealers in the town. Some of these were still lying in his house; by taking one of his donkeys as transport I was able to remove them. Also, a few weavers had sold the wool given out to them so I took this too and they soon cleared up their accounts.

Ziegler staff with local merchants

Winter was very trying physically for the nights were bitterly cold; and there was often much snow, and in daytime the sun was powerful enough to turn the alleys and courtyards into sticky mud. On going into the Djapelakgh district a little later on I encountered a veritable blizzard, taking over two and a half hours to ride six or seven miles arriving at the most wretched of halting places with my right arm encased in ice. However, for a few krans I was offered a perfect specimen of a silver coin of Vonones, Parthian king.

Once we were attacked by some men with sticks and stones, but they soon ran away when a shot was fired over their heads, and we were not molested when returning by the same road. This was the only occasion on which our rifles were actually used; during the time I spent in Iran there were many highway robberies, some with fatal results, but as far as I was concerned no other unpleasant incident occurred.

This winter I inspected altogether 48 villages containing 600 carpet looms. In the following spring we experienced the greatest floods in living memory. Now the water supply of most places is dependent upon underground aqueducts called kanats. Near the top of the alluvial slopes a shaft is dug until water is struck, then some thirty or forty yards lower down another shaft is dug and the two connected underground, and so it goes on, each succeeding shaft being slightly less deep until the water level and ground surface coincide. There, cultivation begins and the village is built. This form of engineering work is carried out without the aid of any instruments.

When the firm bought the ground for our establishment we acquired two-thirds of a kanat, from which a good water supply came, although rather low in dry seasons. This spring's great flood emanated from a tropical downpour lasting sixteen hours. Just outside our compound was a river bed, usually quite dry; a tremendous flood swept along it, overflowing and wrecking the fields carefully laid out for irrigation, penetrating villages, bringing down houses and demolishing all the bridges except the one built by Zieglers. It overflowed also into the shafts of the kanat causing collapse and blockage.

As soon as practicable the 'plumber' responsible for the upkeep of the kanats sent two workmen down to clear the channel, but there must have been another obstruction further up the aqueduct for suddenly the men were swept away by a torrent of mud, stones and water, tearing them from the ropes and tackle to which they were attached. Others lower down manged to grab one man as he was being swept past underground; although he was a mass of bruises and abrasions from head to foot, and nearly drowned, he eventually recovered. The body of the other one was not found for several days. The police tried to make trouble for the master plumber, but we protected him, no further action being taken after some provision was made for the widow.

About this time the firm's premises were constituted a British Vice-Consulate, successive managers becoming honorary Vice-Consuls for many years afterwards. An extraordinary position arose from this arrangement for until about 1912 the manager was a German, the German Legation had made the same arrangement for the German Carpet Company and their first manager was an Englishman. At the outbreak of war in 1914 our man in Sultanabad was English too, so that was the end of German representation in the town.

In early May when fine weather had set in, two of us decided to climb Sefid Kaneh, a 10,000 foot mountain eight miles away. It took us fifteen hours from start to finish; there proved to be hardly any climbing involved, the mountain was merely very steep: with a deal of snow about, the glare from the fierce sun was almost unbearable. Some idea of the extensive view from the summit may be gained by stating in a comparative way that if we had been standing on an eminence in Birmingham we would have been able to see both London and Manchester!

Owing to the heavy spring rains the salt lake had extended enormously and was now about 45 miles in circumference, much of it very shallow and not more than a few inches deep. In the middle there was an island about three miles out; we arranged to explore it but first we had to build a boat. By soaking planks in a pond in the garden, tying them to stakes in a sunny place in the necessary shape, the result was a curious flat-bottomed affair with a small plank on edge as a keel. We also managed to produce a mast and sail. Then it was carried to where a ditch took surplus water from a kanat to the lake and, with some difficulty, launched it and sailed off to the island. The Iranians were convinced that we went there in search of treasure. However, the island was quite featureless, just a raised patch of the usual desert overgrown with the dwarf, very thorny, rose bush *Rosa Persica.* Rowing back against the wind we disturbed vast numbers of flamingos which rose like a pink cloud into the sky.

This spring there was quite a lot of fighting between the various political factions in the town, and the clergy took advantage of this to undermine the position of the Governor, Prince Bahram Mirza, son of the Zil-e-Sultan. Finally the Prince let it be known that he had sent to Isfahan for some cavalry, whereupon the chief mujtahid left the town with two or three hundred followers, mostly seyjids, taking up residence in the holier atmosphere of Kum. Guns were fired off from time to time, one day in fact, to judge from the noise there was a pitched battle going on, but we heard afterwards that the only casualties were one donkey (killed) and one onlooker (slightly wounded).

Iranians have a natural courtesy which makes social contact easy, being great conversationalists and have a keen sense of humour. An old Persian story is a very good illustration of this:

'Once upon a time there lived in Isfahan a great philosopher, known all over the kingdom for his wisdom, but notorious also for his meanness and miserly habits. One day he was followed home by a beggar who begged for alms and refused to be shaken off. At last the philosopher, losing patience turned to him and said: "For your persistence I will give you alms on one condition. Know then that I have an artificial eye of such excellent workmanship that no one can say with certainty which of my eyes is the artificial one. Now if you can tell me which that one is, not merely hazarding a guess but giving a sound reason for your choice, I shall reward you". The beggar gazed into the philosopher's face and said: "Master, it is the right eye which is artificial". "That is correct", said the philosopher, "Now tell me your reason". "Master", said the beggar, "It was the one with the compassionate look in it".'

Hospitality to the traveller is extended as a matter of course, for there is no possible public accommodation; the headman almost invariably put his house at my disposal, even though it often involved considerable inconvenience to himself and his household. Very adequate remuneration was always offered and usually accepted, generally after at least a show of reluctance. The other side of the picture is that you had to keep a close control of your servants and shopkeepers, who extracted the utmost from you, short of actually taking the money out of your pocket. Apart from the eternal vigilance required in matters concerning goods and money, life in Iran could be very pleasant for the European who could adapt himself to the mode of thought and their way of living. How far I was adaptable myself I do not know, but I do know that on the whole I enjoyed my life in Iran and can look back on it with interest and pleasure.

By the time our Sultanabad manager had travelled to Europe to bring his family back from a holiday it was early spring; I was thus free to leave and return to England. Although by this time the country was politically very unsettled and robbers very active, no incident arose to prevent a fairly rapid carriage journey to the Caspian. From Baku I travelled in six days via Berlin to London. After a few months at home I went to the United States on carpet business, and in the following February was sent to Iran for the third time. On the whole, from various points of view, this was the least interesting of all my travels because most of it was done throughout in post carriages, a mode of travel that involves changing horses at every stage. Even by today's standards posting was a costly form of travel, but it had the advantage of comparative speed, if that is the right word to use in connection with this form of traffic. What it amounted to is this – you could go from Teheran to Isfahan, 270 miles, by using a carriage and post horses in four or five days, whereas caravanning, that is of course riding, the journey would take at least a fortnight.

Leonard and Walter Flinn leaving Manchester, 1909

On this occasion I played a more passive role as guide and companion to my father[16], who had somewhat belatedly decided he ought to have a look at the business from the other end. From a business point of view, the trip was of considerable value to him but as an essay in travel it was rather the reverse. He was well over fifty and had led a comfortable and well-appointed life, he disliked the Iranian food, slept badly and was often indisposed. Also, the weather being unusually severe, the discomforts of travel in Iran thereby increased. Already in Vienna we had a foretaste of what was to come when a foot of snow fell during the day and

---

[16] Walter Flinn

a half that we were there; almost as far as Baku we could not see out of the carriage windows on account of continual hard frost and snow, added to which the sole illumination in our railway carriage was one candle. At Rostov both the sea and the Don were frozen over and our carriages were crossing on the ice. The average speed of the train worked out at ten miles per hour and, as there was no dining car, refreshments had to be bought at the stations. But these were excellent, including such things as suckling pigs and crayfish.

From Resht we had a post carriage for the 220 miles to Teheran, it was practically a museum piece. In shape and size not unlike a cab with dirty, tattered upholstery and windows from which the glass had long since disappeared, the interior was so constructed that it was impossible to stretch one's legs. The springs were tightly bound with rope, which may have prevented them from breaking but which also hindered them from exercising the function for which they were designed. Of course there were no lamps or lights of any kind but if you only get one candle in a Russian railway carriage you can hardly expect headlamps on an Iranian cab.

Walter Flinn and carriage near Resht

At first, the road runs through the level coastal strip as far as Menjil where the river Kizil Uzen is crossed by an iron bridge. Spring was well on the way here at the beginning of March: there were many flowers on the road banks, primroses being conspicuous. We drove through the night in pouring rain, the roads being very muddy with everything in the carriage becoming contaminated. Leaving Menjil we came up into mountainous country for we had to ascend several thousand feet to get over the mountain barrier which separates the arid Iranian plateau from the fertile Caspian plain. This chain of mountains serves as a weather fence, south of which precipitation rarely appears between April and December. The roads became heavier the higher we got owing to the snow and heavy rain, eventually getting into deep snow with partially cleared drifts. Stuck at one lonely, dirty posthouse waiting for fresh horses, life seemed a little better, for there was a stove made of old paraffin tins, so we had some soup, eggs, potted meat and Iranian bread plus a last bottle of Russian wine. Sleep was fitful, camel caravans with their huge bells passing continually, and it was 5 a.m. on a clear moonlit morning when we set off again. The mud and slush of the night before had frozen solid making travel very difficult; the vehicles bounced and rocked alarmingly and it was very cold. As the sun rose higher, the roads looked not like roads at all but ploughed fields, and very badly ploughed at that. Finally, through pools of slime, we reached Kasvin. Now we were through the mountains the road improved and we drove along the northern verge of the immense central plain of Iran, the Elburz range on our left hand for all the remaining 90 miles to Teheran.

Such were the efforts needed to penetrate into Iran from the north before the motor car came into its own, bringing with it a vast improvement in roads all over the country, but that era only opened some 15 years later. Long before we got there my father had discarded any romantic notions he might have had about travelling in Iran.

We did not stay long in Teheran, business being more or less at a standstill on account of an unsettled political situation.

Travelling on uneventfully to Isfahan, we had a great welcome from the merchant community and several large parties were organised. Fortunately we had a very large room and I wish I had been able to take a picture of the forty or so pairs of shoes on the threshold. Iranians always take them off before entering a room: as I have never heard of a theft of shoes on such an occasion it must be one of those things which are definitely not done. Our chief official visit was to the Governor, a tall striking-looking man with a rugged countenance. He had naturally quite a lot to say about political affairs, notably that whilst he was aware of the agreement between Russia and England about Iran, he knew perfectly well that English sympathies were with the constitutionalists and that the Russians were helping the Shah, a delicate distinction in the measure of support afforded by the two countries to their favoured parties.

When the Governor, also the leader of the Bakhtiari tribes, heard that we were leaving shortly for Sultanabad he became rather worried for he assumed that we were contemplating the direct caravan road which all the way runs close to Bakhtiari country, and his own tribesmen were constantly making raids on caravans. But when he was told that we were not going that way, but by Kashan and Kum: he cheered up and said that he was sure that we would find a more comfortable route. On our return from this visit to him we found a telegram from our Shiraz manager saying that he had been robbed on his way to Isfahan and had to return to Shiraz, having nothing left but what he stood up in; not even that as we subsequently heard.

It was a much better spring at Sultanabad than in the previous year and the gardens were gay with flowers, all coming out together, clumps of snapdragons flowering simultaneously with daffodils, tulips and iris. Most impressive were the long rows of tall fritillaries, the crown imperial variety. Many of the wild flowering dwarf iris were represented, among them a rare white one. I found it in a narrow valley a couple of miles away, the Mowdarreh, just poking its blooms up on the surface of a scree slope. Our stay here was more or less a holiday for me so I made many short excursions, climbing the Sefid Khaneh again. It was pleasant too to pay visits to some of the villages in the role of a guest rather than that of a taskmaster; my father was called the sahib-buzurk, the big master, whereas I was known as the sahab-kuchik, little master, and in our offices peser-e-sharik, or son of the partner. One day, some of the staff sailed over to the island but a gale sprang up and they had to walk the last mile to the shore, pushing the boat in a few inches of water and over a foot of mud. They arrived home deadbeat, caked to the eyebrows with mud and salt.

In Hamadan there was quite an antique market, rare coins being often imitated very cleverly, especially the gold coins of the Sassanian period. The chief source of finds of antique pottery and coins was at the northern end of the Sultanabad plain; in one area the ground is smooth with bits of terracotta and fragments of pottery. Evidently there was a big settlement here which was probably destroyed by the Mongols, for such coins as found are all before the time of the Timur in the thirteenth century.

After an uneventful return to Teheran, we found that the political situation had become more complicated, it looked as if civil war must develop. The Shah had got his troops together and an army had left the capital en route for Kasvin. The revolutionists were between the latter town and the Caspian, not having moved much further towards Teheran since we passed two months before. The army also appeared to be in no great hurry and were encamped near Kerej, about fifteen miles from the town. This meant that we had to pass through both forces to reach the Caspian again. Through an Iranian friend we obtained a testimonial of our reliability for the revolutionary people and from official sources a 'laissez passer' to use with the Shah's army. However, beyond asking if we carried any arms, neither side displayed much curiosity about us, which was just as well as we had a bag of around 500 roubles in gold, wrapped in some old sacking under the seat of the carriage which we were taking to Baku. This was perfectly legitimate, but we might have arrived there with a receipt for 500 roubles, or without even that, instead of the cash.

The climax in Iran came shortly after our return to Manchester. Mohammed Ali Shah was forced to abdicate in favour of his small son Sultan Ahmed, and retire into exile. Meanwhile, the country, having asserted itself, soon relapsed into a condition very little different to what it had been before the revolution. An epoch-making event, and one that had tremendous influence on the future of the country, was the discovery of oil in south west Iran seven years after the granting of a concession to an Englishman called D'Arcy, by Muzzafer-e-Din Shah. The present standing of the Anglo-Iranian Oil Company and the fact that the British government holds 51% of its shares reflects the importance of the discovery, both from an economic and a political point of view. That our government is now intimately concerned with it is both a source of strength and weakness to the oil company, strength because in time of war, the protection of the government is certain, which would certainly not be the case if it were a private trading concern, and weakness because of necessity under these conditions, its hands are tied by political considerations. But perhaps it is neither necessary nor tactful to elaborate this theme.

In 1914, after several years of ups and downs, a certain amount of progress had been achieved and I was contemplating another tour when war broke out, so until 1919 I was otherwise engaged.

Chapter 7

After the Great War

'Patience is the gate of joy; haste is the gate of repentance'

During the first World War Iran had declared its neutrality, but no belligerent took the declaration seriously. In fact the Russians moved into Tabriz shortly after the war broke out. Later on the Turks appeared and the Russians retired from Tabriz but the town changed hands more than once. The Turks also entered the country by way of Kermanshah and fighting ensued on Iranian territory, the British being involved as well as the Russians. Elsewhere in Iran there were bands of German armed propagandists and their Iranian sympathisers who were able to force all British subjects out of Isfahan and Sultanabad. Generally speaking they did not loot and did little or no damage to our property and possessions, while the Russians, who eventually caused them to flee from these towns, stole a great deal of stuff in Sultanabad including many fine carpets.

In Shiraz all non-German Europeans were taken prisoner by tribesmen and held for a long time not far from Bushire, itself held by the British. The Shah's neutrality (he was a mere youth at the time) was a very frail thing, he had been persuaded by a German coterie to leave Teheran with them for the south and was only prevented at the last moment, almost by force, by the British and Russian ministers.

After the war, in 1920, those parts of the country not actually occupied by foreign troops relapsed into a very disorganised state, road robberies became more frequent and insurance premiums rose to uneconomic heights, war risk being quoted as 10%.

Altogether by the end of the year the internal state of Iran seemed almost hopeless. Both postal and telegraphic communications were bad, so it was under these conditions in the autumn that I began to make arrangements to undertake another tour. The only possible route was via the Gulf, and passages were very difficult to obtain. Eventually I got a berth on the P.& O. 'Caledonia' to Bombay without any guarantee that I would there be able to transfer to a steamer going up the Gulf. I was officially informed too that I travelled on my own responsibility, that my journey was depreciated and that I could not be allowed to travel by Basra and Baghdad. I did venture to point out that it was precisely because things were in such a state of flux that someone with authority was going out to take decisions on the spot, but no further communication was received. As I already had passport and visas, without further ado I departed.

A radio message to Bushire the day before I arrived permitted me to go by Baghdad after all. It transpired that a train of empty cattle trucks was about to go there on a trial trip and the R.T.O. (officer in charge) kindly allowed me the use of one truck for myself on the payment of a first class fare. There was nothing in the truck, a box car of the '40 hommes, 8 chevaux' type, except evidence of the previous tenants, but I made myself fairly comfortable with a camp bed and my luggage. Starting at midnight, at about 8 a.m. we came to Ur where Abraham was born, but I wished I was in Manchester where I was born, after a night made hideous by the jangling and clatter of about half a mile of iron trucks. Greatly to my surprise an orderly came along and told me breakfast was ready, so I went to the little station building where a substantial English breakfast was put before me. At a station further along the line hordes of Arab passengers tried to board the train but were not permitted to, on the grounds that there was no third class accommodation for them. Apparently only first class passengers were allowed to travel in cattle trucks. At Samawa an Indian stationmaster asked me whether I had a ticket, and when I produced my first class one he said the hire of the cattle truck cost more than that, and I must pay the difference. Knowing full well whose pocket this would go to I referred him to a place even hotter than Samawa in summer time, and he did not carry the argument any further. Happily an officer joined me in my very hot tin cabin bearing with him a bottle of whisky, which I lacked. But I had plenty of soda water, of which he had none, so the end of the day saw our stocks very low.

At Baghdad I found letters describing the latest revolution in Iran. Under their commanding officer, Reza Khan, the Persian Cossack Regiment had suddenly swept into Teheran. They arrested many members of the Majless (parliament) as they could find. A Royalist-Constitutionalist government had been formed and the editor of a Teheran newspaper, Seyd Zia, was appointed Prime Minister with plenary powers. Otherwise the situation remained calm. At first glance, this might have been merely the transfer from one set of men to another but as time moved on it became evident that this coup d'état was in fact the end of ramshackle Persia and the birth of modern Iran.

'Tin Lizzie'

The rest of the journey to Teheran was now to be by car, a new mode of transport in Iran for me. From Kermanshah onwards this was a Ford of the 'Tin Lizzie' variety bought second-hand especially for me. So on March 14th, Mr Hutton, our Sultanabad manager, and I left in threatening weather and before we reached Bisitun it was pouring with rain. Soon the car began to go wrong and we stuck on a pass called Bid-e-Surkh or Red Willow. Coolies clearing the road pushed us up and we went along alright until we started up the Asadabad pass, about ninety miles from Kermanshah, so we dropped back to the village and stayed the night with the officer in charge of the road. Next day, after various adjustments we again attempted the pass but couldn't get much further than the previous night and had perforce to stay a second one in

Asadabad. Next day we got some of the way up, and with the help of ten men we managed to reach the top. The mud was awful, the snowfall having been tremendously heavy, there were in places walls of snow thirty feet high. We ploughed our way down through seas of slush and mud, the engine performing as if the spirit of a recalcitrant mule had entered into it. We only got over the pass just in time for it soon began to snow again for two days. All roads had become impassable for wheeled traffic and we had to abandon the idea of motoring any further.

Hamadan, as the ancient Ecbatana, was supposed to have had a Jewish colony since the days of the captivity and there are still a number of Jews there, as indeed there are in a number of other large Iranian towns. Just as in the rest of the world they had been segregated and persecuted from time to time; by now animosity had died down as it had also towards the Armenians. The Iranians have a saying that it takes three Iranians to cheat a Jew and three Jews to cheat an Armenian. I rather think that an Iranian would consider himself the equal of three Englishmen in this respect so obviously we must start at a considerable disadvantage in dealing with the other two races.

But the office servants and horses belonging to our Sultanabad establishment were at Hamadan and so available for our onward journey. On our first day's ride we only managed to cover twelve miles towards what appeared to be a clump of igloos but which turned out to be the village of Murad Bulaghi. We had to stumble through seas of mud, rock and snowdrifts, snow falling all the time, and as soon as we arrived a blizzard broke loose. There was no military road and no one attempted to clear the snow. I was well below par with jaundice although I did not know it at the time, moreover I had not ridden for twelve years. Still, with a weather-proof little mud room, our camp beds, a fire and a good meal of rice and eggs we managed to forget our misery for a time. Four more days of this kind of riding found us in Sultanabad.

Again, after a two night rest we left here in the Ford which had caught up with us, the road having been reported in good condition. This proved to be the case; however at one point a wheel came off and further on the gearbox shed all its oil and we had none with us. We put in a lump of roghan (clarified fat) and a tin of grease and by this way we ran the fifty miles to Teheran, ruining the big ends in the process. Apart from this there were no incidents. It is amazing how one could treat these 'Tin Lizzies' and still get through.

The situation was greatly improved from all points of view except from that of the previous holders of power. A radical revolution had taken place, but there had been no liquidation. That system of reform would have been repugnant to the Iranians, it was introduced later by nations which considered themselves on a higher grade of civilisation. Nevertheless many ministers, governors of towns and provinces and other officials, who had used their offices and positions to amass wealth for themselves, were seized and imprisoned. By disgorging a considerable portion of their ill-gotten gains, most of them regained their freedom fairly soon. It was the system that was rotten rather than the men, for most posts were farmed out to the highest bidder, naturally each one making as much as he could for himself. The population accepted the changed regime with equanimity, and the new cabinet proceeded with its schemes for reform with Reza Khan as Minister of War.

Business had been at a standstill for several months, for a great many traders had sent their goods away and were now engaged in getting them back. Gradually a few branches of trade began to revive, and in several places we began to get busy again with carpet and rug purchases for American customers. So I arranged to go to Isfahan; the Ford had been thoroughly overhauled and was in reasonably good condition but I had reckoned without the weather. It had become much warmer and enormous masses of snow were melting rapidly, flooding every available road, even the desert road used by camel drivers – "Kavir bala amad" (the swamp had risen) said the camel drivers.

After many false starts eventually I went off on horseback and rode all the way to Isfahan. One day, when I had been riding for some time and was beginning to wonder where the next village was, I met a man riding on a donkey. He said that the village of Bughin was quite close by, in fact "yek sedai khurus" (a cock-crow) away. On the last day, a fine sight on the high lying desert beyond Dilijan were the masses of eremurus, a plant which has a single spike of flowers of a pale apricot hue, about three feet tall and with a peach-like smell. I cut an armful to decorate the house and took a few roots for the garden.

A week in Isfahan sufficed for what had to be done. I went on to Shiraz by carriage, passing on the way a colossal caravan of camels; eighteen miles of them, over 7000. In the town, our house had been refurbished after the wartime looting. I was rather nonplussed when I went to have dinner with two of the officers of the South Persia Rifles to see two of our carpets on the floor. The Kashgais had taken them from our house, sold them in the bazaar and they had been bought in the usual way for the mess. Most disconcerting.

The British had nearly completed a motor road to Bushire over the passes but there were no cars for civilians in any case, so I had to ride, this time on a mule which turned out to be a most satisfactory animal. Owing to the late rains the desert vegetation was now at its best and some hillsides looked like gigantic rock gardens. Patches of red oriental poppies, purple larkspur, bushes of white flowers like convolvulus; also hollyhocks and many other flowers which do not grow wild in England.

At Konar Takhteh I met a young Indian English army officer who was writing a report of a brush that he had had with a body of men who had attacked his small force from an old fort. There was a passage in the report which even I, with small knowledge of military matters, knew might have caused him instant recall and even earned him a bowler hat. So we put our heads together and glossed over the doubtful incident: I believe it was accepted without question when I handed it over, sealed of course, to the competent authority in Bushire. He certainly seemed possessed of courage and initiative and I hope he became a general.

At Bushire I heard that Seyd Zia's cabinet had fallen and he had fled to Baghdad. Various reasons were given for this, some said he tried to introduce too many unpopular reforms, others that he had refused to agree to corrupt practices on the part of the Shah. The real reason was, no doubt, Reza Khan's own ambition, which consistently carried him on to greater power. How that culminated is now a matter of history and requires no elaboration in a record such as this sets out to be. Reza Khan's rise continued and he became Prime Minister in 1923. In view of his strong personality and his hold over the army, the Shah, Sultan Ahmed, became a mere puppet and very soon left for Europe from whence he never returned. Later, a plan was devised whereby Iran was to become a republic with Reza Khan as President, but it provoked such general hostility, fermented by the mujtahids, that it was dropped. Nevertheless Reza Khan remained as a virtual dictator and in 1925 the Shah was deposed and the crown offered to Reza Khan who accepted it. The coronation took place almost exactly five years to the day since he, as colonel of the Cossack brigade, had executed his coup d'état.

All the main roads in the country were reconstructed: the method appears to have been the eminently simple one of digging two parallel ditches and depositing the excavated material between them, the latter then being covered with a gravelling material. Broad avenues were driven through the towns with little or no compensation to the owners whose properties were destroyed or damaged. Factories for cotton, wool, sugar and other products were built, even for cigarettes and beer. The latter was quite good although the quality was liable to vary, and as for the cigarettes, I soon got to prefer them to English Virginian. The administration of law and education, which had been largely dispensed by the mullahs, was taken away from them as soon as the Shah felt himself strong enough to do so. He had never liked the clergy and took every opportunity to diminish their powers.

The long-projected railway was put in hand, its alignment revised so that it began and ended on Iranian soil, and for this purpose two new terminal ports were created: Bandar Shah on the Caspian Sea and Bandar Shahpur on the Gulf. It was during this period also that British textiles suffered a decline, which in the end amounted to virtual extinction. They were supplanted by Russian, Indian and, above all, by Japanese production. Japanese prints were sold at prices which in Lancashire the British exporter had to pay for printing alone. Several companies, including our own, turned their attention to motor transport and started service stations in various towns. For a long time, we acted as distributing agents for the oil company's petrol. Subsequently, the latter took over this part of the business themselves, erecting petrol pumps all over the country, whereas, when we were handling the business, the sole means of distribution was the four gallon tin.

From the outset of the new Shah's reign two main principles became clear. One was Iran for the Iranians; any sort of control or interference in Iranian affairs by other countries was to be got rid of at once, and this was achieved pretty quickly. Only a determined and ruthless man like Shah Reza could have hastened the process to such a degree that one really felt that things were on the move. In 1921, for instance, one stood a fair chance of being held up almost anywhere, whereas by 1930 when I went out for the fifth time one could travel all over the country without fear of molestation.

I secured a passage to Bombay where I joined the P.&O. 'Malwa' for a pleasant if somewhat sultry voyage through the Red Sea to Suez and Marseilles. Though of course I could not know it at the time I had said goodbye to old Persia. No more was I to spend days and weeks riding slowly from town to town and from village to village: by the time I returned again cars, trucks and planes had superseded horses, mules and camels. Nevertheless, had I not had the opportunities of experiencing the age-old method of travel, I would not have gained an insight into the Persian ways of life and thought, nor should I have appreciated the immense progress and rapid transition from Persia as it had been for centuries to the modern Iran as we know it.

Chapter 8

Fifth Journey, 1930 and World War II

'The eye of a needle is large enough for two friends but the whole world's too small for two enemies'

The character of the business had changed completely by the time I returned to Teheran in 1930. The cotton piece goods trade had disappeared, throttled out of existence by competition from other countries, chiefly Japan whose selling prices were incredibly low. These of course must have been in due relation with the cost of production, for the great Japanese merchant firms amassed large fortunes, but by our standards their factory worker did not get much of a share in this prosperity. On the other hand, the motor transport industry had developed enormously, for many roads had been constructed; goods could be distributed all over the country by transport services from India, Russia, Iraq and from the Gulf. A steady deterioration in the rate of exchange made imported goods and vehicles difficult to pay for and many contracts were repudiated. Other obstacles to the free flow of trade also arose.

Such was the improvement in the roads that I was able to visit all our branches by car, the journeys between the towns taking a number of hours rather than the days or weeks or travel on horseback or the horse carriage of my early sojourns. A few days in each place from Bushire in the South to Tabriz in the North sufficed for my business purposes.

Outward I had travelled by the sea route – overland to Marseilles, then through the Mediterranean and Red Seas to Bombay and eventually the Gulf. Now I decided to return, for a change, overland by rail as far as possible.

Tajir's train in Iraq

Through the ubiquitous Thomas Cook & Sons I was able to book right through from Baghdad to London. Leaving Baghdad at night, next morning found me at Kirkuk, still in Iraq where cars were waiting to take us on to Mosul. Here we stayed overnight in a railway rest house, going on to Nisibin the following day. At this point we met the rail track again and a train was drawn up outside the station although we were not allowed to board it for several hours. It had a sleeping car, and the guard cooked meals somehow in his van, serving them in the compartments. They were surprisingly good.

At Charchemish we saw Hittite carvings still lying on the station where they had been left years before by some German expedition. I think they must have served as models for those which decorate the building of London Transport at Broadway, S.W.1. Two hours stop at Aleppo gave us the opportunity for a quick drive round the town. Undoubtedly the slow climb next morning through the Cilician Gates is the outstanding feature of the entire railway trip across Asia Minor. At places the track seems to be on a ledge on the cliff-like sides of a steep gorge, until the gorge itself suddenly emerges on to the vast monotonous interior plain. After another night we awoke to find that we were running down a pleasant mountain valley to the shore of the Sea of Marmora.

We had no time for sightseeing on this occasion in Stamboul[17] for the Orient Express left the same afternoon. I left at

Lausanne for a couple of days walking in the Jura Mountains, completing my journey by normal rail services.

For a time, the firm held its own but various happenings combined to make its existence impossible. The pound went off the gold standard followed by the dollar, thus depreciating the value of large stocks held in Iran, for they became replaceable at a lower cost in Iranian currency. Further, an ordinance was enacted in Iran whereby it was made compulsory for exporters to sell to the Government, at the official rate of exchange, all the foreign currency derived from exports, thus depriving the firm of a means of realising payments received from sales in the country. In 1934, therefore, the firm of Ziegler & Co. was compelled to close down and withdraw from Iran. It had started operations in that country in the 1860s, so after 75 years its passing was regretted by a large number of merchants and friends.

Many radical changes were brought about by the Shah's regime, such as the completion of the railway and the re-planning of the towns; there was other evidence of an advance towards Western culture. Cinemas, railways and motor cars accorded ill with the traditional garb of Iran. A new form of headgear for men was devised, somewhat similar to a France officer's kepi, and the wearing of it was made compulsory, though it never became general in country

---

[17] Istanbul

districts. Subsequently all men had to wear European attire, and finally women were ordered to discard the veil and also wear European clothes. This last measure proved rather difficult to enforce as large numbers of women did not appear to yearn for this form of emancipation. Buses, carriages and taxis were forbidden to accept women as passengers unless they wore European clothes. The wives of thousands of government employees had to call on pay day for their husband's wages, they went away empty handed if they were not wearing European dress.

The press formed a subservient chorus, it could scarcely indeed have done anything else under what was virtually a dictatorship. It improved upon the Shah's lead and was violently anti-foreign, its choicest abuse being reserved for Britain in general and the Anglo-Iranian Oil Company[18] in particular. Perhaps I ought to state that I am not a shareholder in that or any other business. I might have been had Ziegler & Co. responded to Mr D'Arcy's[19] invitation to co-operate in his original operations. As a junior in the firm at the time I was unaware of this matter until I found his letter years later amongst some old papers.

---

[18] The Anglo-Iranian Oil Company became British Petroleum in 1954.
[19] See Page 81

By 1939 the Shah's popularity had waned considerably although this was not perceptible from the tone of the press. He had become enormously wealthy, more autocratic and brooked no opinion other than his own. He was said to have behaved violently on occasions towards his own ministers. Nevertheless, in spite of having acquired in a large measure 'les défauts de ses qualités' he will still rank in history as one of the great rulers of Iran.

By an Iranian friend I was told the following story of the Shah when he was a boy of 13, "Of course it may not be true – but as he told the story to me, I will tell it unto you". He and his father were walking in the palace garden and were about to go indoors. As they reached the door the boy started to go in before the father. The Shah restrained him, saying "My son, you must never do that, I must always go first, for I am the Shah and a greater man than you are". The boy thought a moment, then said, "No, father, you are wrong, it is I who am the greater man". "How did you make that out" asked the Shah. "Well", said his son, "MY father is a shah". Se non e vero.

During World War II I was lucky enough to have a final chance to travel around Iranian towns and villages once more. Believe it or not, I was considered fit enough, despite a surfeit of birthdays, to be a P.R. Officer for the Ministry of Information Bureau at Teheran. My eighteen months tour of duty ended in the autumn of 1944, forty one years to the day after the start of my first journey[20].

I will never see Iran again, for the time is approaching when travelling will become a wearying effort instead of a pleasurable activity. And so, in the same surroundings as it was conceived, I bring my rambling tale to an end. A full moon is shining on the foothills and the Lakeland fells loom faintly in the distance, giving the illusion that I am looking out from the rooftop of some village in Iran. But I have come down from the hill to my room, for one does not sleep on the roof in Grange-over-Sands.

Grange-over-Sands

1955

---

[20] One might speculate that Tajir's last tour in Iran could have been linked to the Teheran conference of November 1943, attended by Churchill, Stalin and Roosevelt.

Songs of Iran
by Tajir

Designed and illustrated
by Paul M. Flinn
with an introduction by
Professor Michael W. Flinn MA, D Lit.

Songs of Iran by 'Tajir'

Introduction

'Tajir' was the pseudonym of my father Leonard Flinn (1882-1971), a Manchester merchant whose business took him to Persia many times between 1903 and 1944. The small Manchester firm, in which his father had been a partner before him, imported carpets from Persia and exported there anything the Persians would buy – mostly cotton goods in the early days, but more miscellaneous goods, including cars, in later times. The firm failed to survive the depression of the early 1930s, and Tajir's last trip to Persia during the second World War was in government service as an official of the Ministry of Information.

In the early years of the present century, travel to and within Persia was not something to be undertaken lightly. To get there involved many days of tedious train and steamer journeys and took him on occasion to the Ruritanian confusion of the pre-1914 Balkans, across the vast expanses of Czarist Russia, and brought him into contact with the uncertainties of the old Turkish imperial regime. Within Persia transport was by horse or mule. Carpets were bought directly from the weavers in villages scattered over many parts of the country, and a carpet buyer's trade involved horseback journeys of many hundreds of miles across hot, dry desert country, with nights spent in inns and caravanserais of a degree of primitiveness that was a far cry from the luxuries of Western Europe. Between the wars these journeys became easier with the advent of the motor car, although it was later still before Persia was able to build roads that made motoring something less than an adventure. On his last visit to Persia, Tajir travelled by plane.

Besides being hardy and athletic – essential qualities for the traveller in early twentieth century Persia–Tajir was a cultured man. Education in Germany and Switzerland gave him a foundation of languages which proved invaluable to him in his extensive travels. In the East he quickly picked up a working knowledge of Persian to add to his French and German. He read extensively about this history and archeology of Persia, acquiring a valuable library of books about the country and making himself an authority on Persian history and culture which was to lead to membership of the Royal Geographical Society and honorary membership of the Iranian Society in London. It was, above all, his affection for the beauty of the country and the romance of its history and legends that prompted him, both at odd moments in his travels, and later in the leisure of retirement, to write about Persia.

There are some fascinating descriptions amongst his papers of journeys in the Persian deserts and mountains in the early part of the century……. But it was, above all, the following collection of poems that best reveal his affection for a land and people whose charms were subtle but, for Tajir at least, enduring.

Professor Michael W. Flinn   MA, D Litt

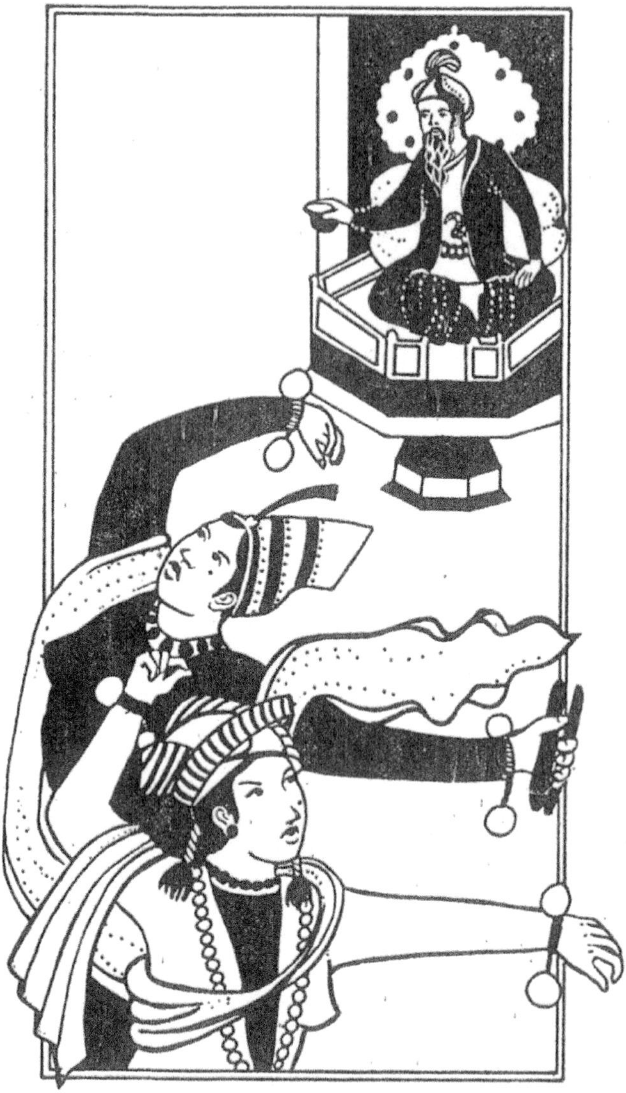

Shiraz

The little rill of Ruknabad,
How pleasantly it flows
Adown the strait of God-is-great,
To meet the Shiraz rose.

The Shiraz rose, the cypress dark
The orange tree aglow,
Where Hafiz and where Sadi sang,
Ah me, how long ago!

And old Omar, who loved his wine
And women too, and song,
All these to praise, he spent his days,
Say, shall we count him wrong?

But these brave days are past and gone,
Their muse, like them, takes wing,
A bleaker air blows through the world
And men no longer sing.

Though few there be whose memory yet
The age of song recalls,
Still chants the little nightingale
Above the mouldering walls.

Let me but pace the garden gay
Therein their laughter ran,
So shall I find some kindred mind,
Where care-free poets sang?

The little rill of Ruknabad,
How pleasantly it flows
Adown the strait of God-is-great,
To meet the Shiraz rose.

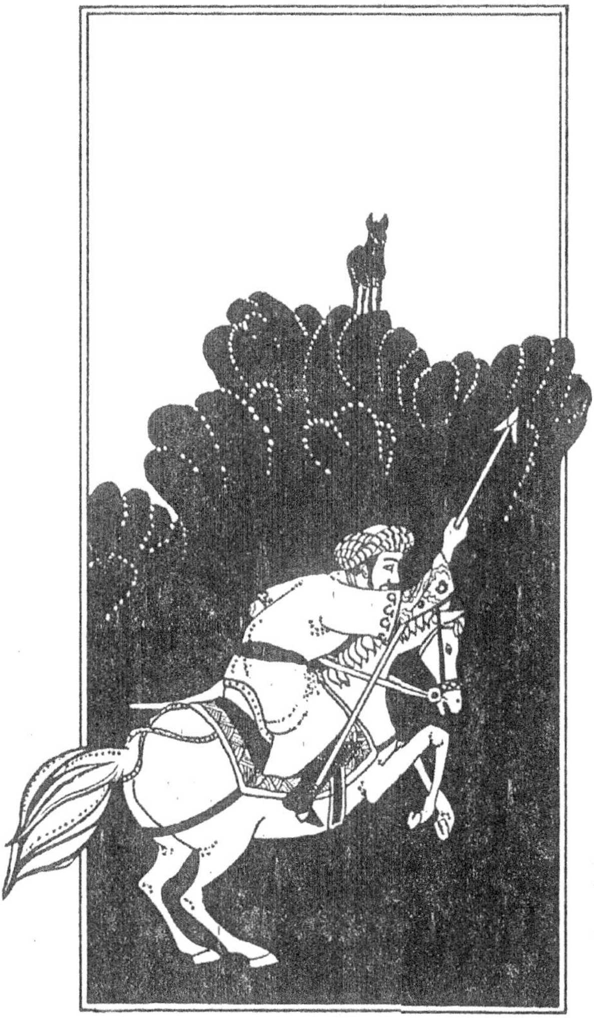

Bahram Gur

Ho, saddle the steed, bring the spear and the bow,

The King goes a-hunting today.

Who rides with his overlord early must rise,

And by starlight set out on his way:

For Bahram the Hunter, the great Bahram Gur,

Is up and away ere the dawn,

And little recks he of the shadows of light,

King Bahram's the herald of morn.

Choose the swiftest of steeds, bring the bravest of men,

And the surest of marksmen that run,

The wild ass, the quarry, will hold out the chase

From the dawn to the setting of sun.

See the golden rays flood all the desert with light,

And fleeting like shadows of grey,

And swifter than deer flies the ass o'er the plain,

Will his speed save the quarry today?

Over sand, over rock, up the crest, down the hill,

Pursued and pursuer fly on,

Midst the gathering heat with its shimmering haze,

Till the morning and mid-day are gone.

Bahram gallops alone, none may hold to his pace,

His steed, peerless, fiery and strong

Has left all behind in its swift-footed stride,

To close with the victim ere long.

Far out on the plain lies the slumbering marsh,

King Bahram, King Bahram, beware,

Where the wild ass may skim o'er the treacherous green,

No horse with its rider may dare.

Yet heedless of danger he draws to the kill,

The quarry at last 'neath his spear,

But the cruel morass open out to their tread,

And hunter and horse disappear.

Where Persepolis' pillars trace fingers of light,
On the heavens, the queen waits alone
Within the vast halls of the palaces proud,
Till the chase of her liege lord be done,

Lamenting aloud see the messengers come,
And bow low before her and say
'Thy son, gracious queen, is now lord of Iran,
'Twas King Bahram's last hunting today.'

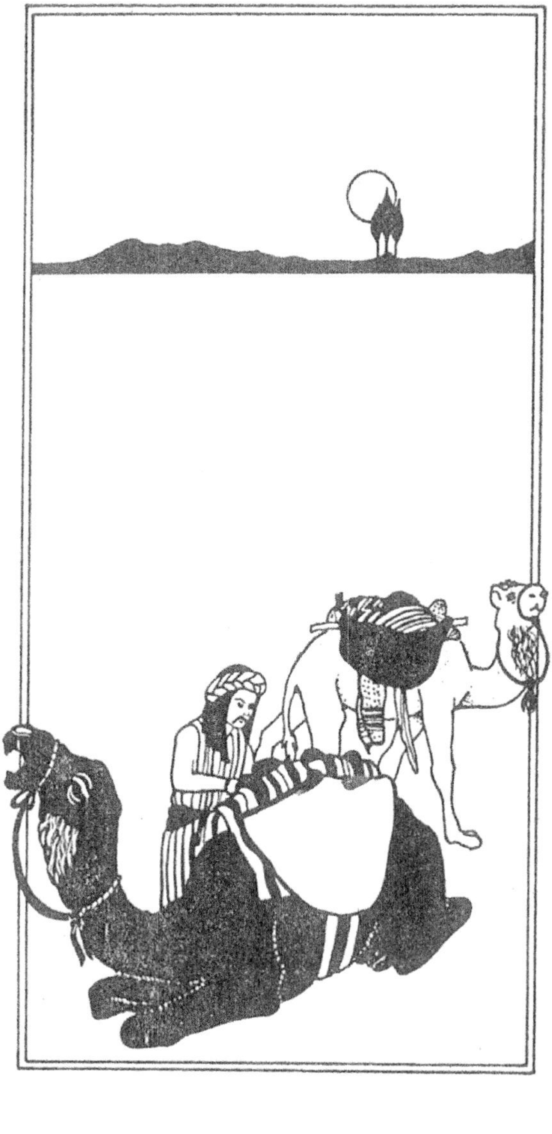

Caravan

Across the desert's dusty space I ride,
My caravan crawls wearily behind,
Rider and beast athirst go stumbling on,
So Allah wills, we'll rest at eventide.

Long, long ago in that dim far-off time,
When Babylon was great, and Britain's realm
Yet but a land scarce dreamt of, out beyond
The ken of nations in their glittering prime,

This plain was noisy with the sound of arms,
Horse, chariot and archer stormed this way,
Persian and Mede united in their might,
Crashed upon empire deaf to war's alarms.

Resistless as the bore in Bristol's bay,
Down from their craggy heights the avenging hordes
Swept o'er Irak, yet now, like Babylon
And Nineveh, their pomp had passed away.

Here in their wake, I march, but nought is found,
No sign of empire, e'en of human life;
A clump of poplars on the desert's rim,
Alone appears to break the empty round.

Yonder where Jemshyd's vaulted halls once stood,
The bearded bulls glare out across the plain,
Gone is the pompous pageantry of might,
O'er mud-built hovels silently they brood.

And here I rest, and with the rising moon
Climb the great stairway to the shattered fanes;
Land of an unforgotten past, arise,
Thy glory sleeps in newer empires' noon.

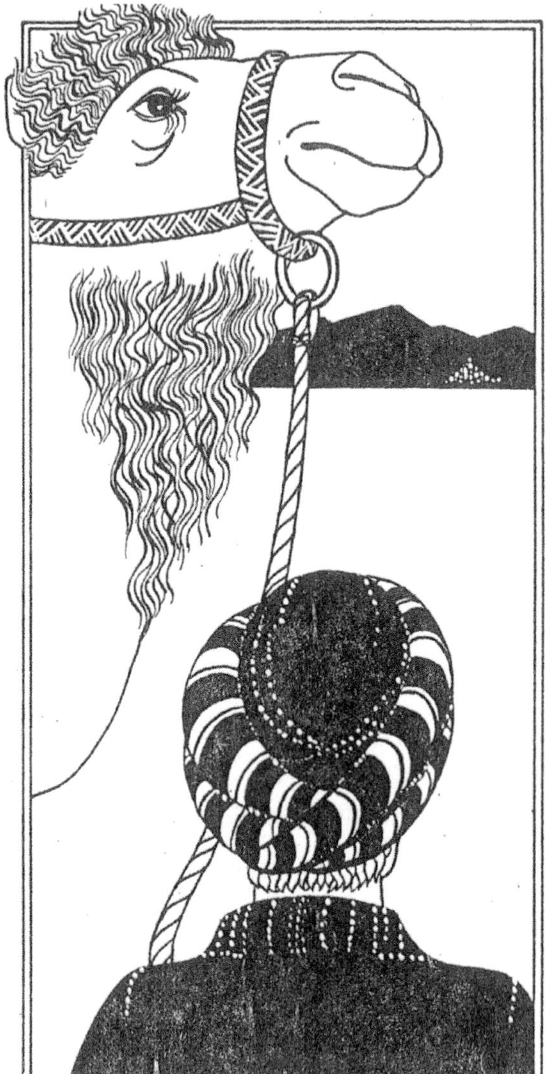

Demavend

At Kum the mosque of Fatima
with glowing golden dome,
And slender minaretted towers,
betokens rest and home
To many a weary caravan
that winds across the plain,
Or haven for a fleeting hour,
ere journeying on again.

Far, far away on Demavend
the summer streaks of snow
Shine pallid in the sunlight,
at eve with crimson glow.
When all else lies in darkness,
that topmost peak of light
Gleams like a rosy lantern
to usher in the night.

'Tis twenty parasangs and more
from Kum to Demavend,
The giant glittering sentinel
that marks the journey's end,
But ere the fretted minarets escape
the wanderer's gaze,
Stands forth that wond'rous mountain peak
till lost in sunset haze.

And through the gloom the live-long night
the clanging camel bells
Ring out across the salty waste
to break the demon spells,
And at the halting-place
upon the desert shore at dawn
Scarce nearer rises Demavend,
lit by the rose red morn.

But onward, ever onward,
by day 'neath brassy skies,
The goal draws near and nearer still,
until the weary eyes
Behold the emerald gardens' gleam,
ringed round with desert brown,
And nestling 'neath the snowy peaks
there stands at last the town.

So when life's little caravan
sets forth from sheltering dome,
May Allah's hand be over you
until the last long home,
For though in burning desert lie
your way unto the end,
Be sure He'll set some peak to guide
like silver Demavend.

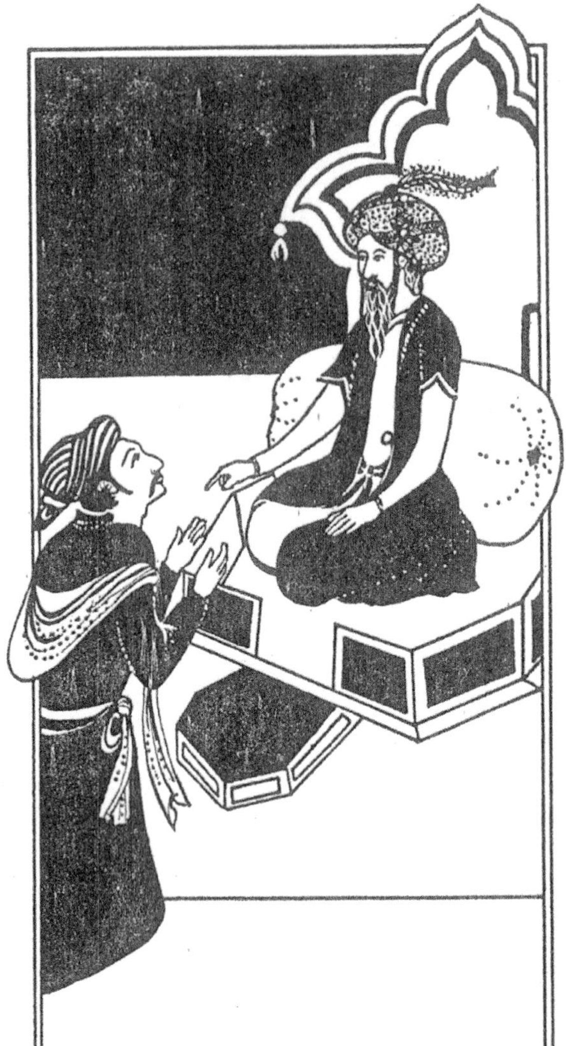

Haji Ibrahim

The vizier Haji Ibrahim,
A man of great renown,
Had planted his relations
In every Persian town.

His nephews were all governors,
And eke his brothers too,
And likewise all the lesser lights
Of Haji Ibrahim's crew.

To him that sat in Isfahan
There came a merchant glum,
Who said "your rates are far too high,
I cannot pay the sum."

"Well, well", replied the governor,
"Unless you pay the fees,
You'll have to leave the neighbourhood,
And live elsewhere at ease."

"To Kashan or to Shiraz go,"
"Not so", replied the man,
"Your nephews both are governors
Of Shiraz and Kazan".

"Then go to Teheran, and tell
The Shah your case is clear,"
"But there again", the merchant said,
"Your brother is vizier."

This quite enraged the governor,
Who roughly answered, "Well,
I've had enough of all this talk,
You'd better go to hell."

"But pardon me, in vain I'd go,"
The witty merchant said,
"Your father, Haji Mirhum, is
Since quite a twelvemonth, dead."

Then laughed out loud the governor
And said, no longer vexed,
"Since my relations interfere,
In this world and the next,

You may now leave this court unscathed
And set your mind at ease,
Your ready wit has saved your purse,
'Tis I will pay your fees".

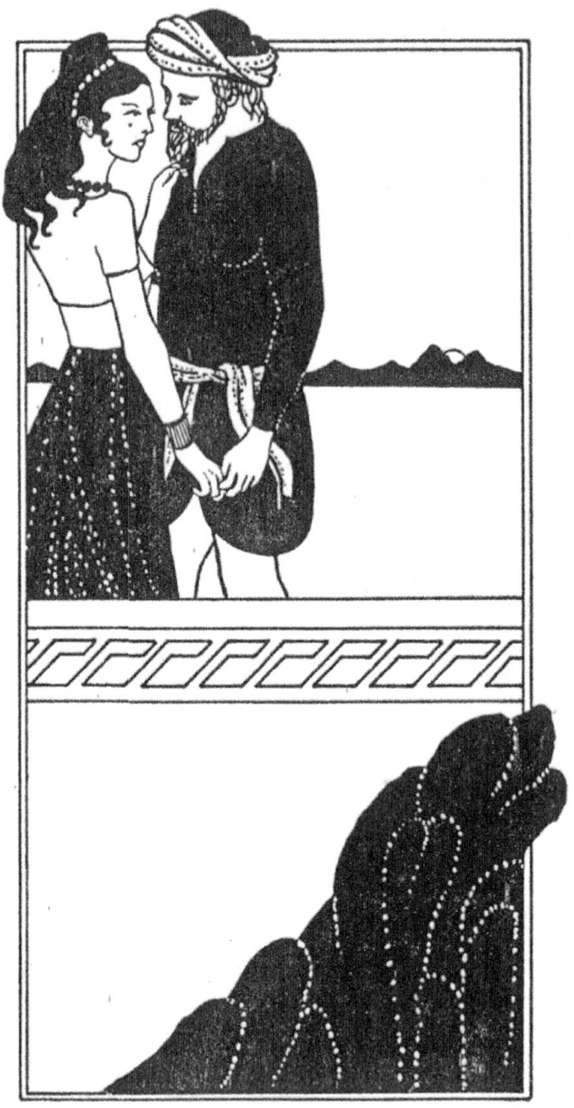

Kasr I Dokhtar

High o'er the pass there frowns a crag,
Where walls and bastions cling,
Though ruined now, they once embraced
A love, which men still sing.

Across the swirling river's flood,
Pent in by rock-bound shore,
A bridge is flung, that all may pass
Unscathed through safety's door.

In olden times, the story runs,
There dwelt upon the height
A princess fair, whose shepherd love
Stole through the flood by night.

And ere the dawn had flushed the peaks
To pinnacles of rose,
He hastened through the stream once more,
His love in triumph grows.

"And does thou nightly stake thy life
At hazard of the tide?
No longer shalt thou thus endure
Such dangers for thy bride".

"Behold across the stream I'll build
A bridge with arches three,
So that thou might securely pass,
My shepherd, love, to me."

And thus she spake, the bridge arose,
Still standing to this day;
How lightly now the shepherd lad
May tread, the lover's way.

Alas, alas for loving heart,

Alas for beauty rare,

The love that nightly braved the flood,

Died, when it might not dare.

Deserted by her lover base,

Her love to canker grown,

Despairing on her castled height

The princess died, alone.

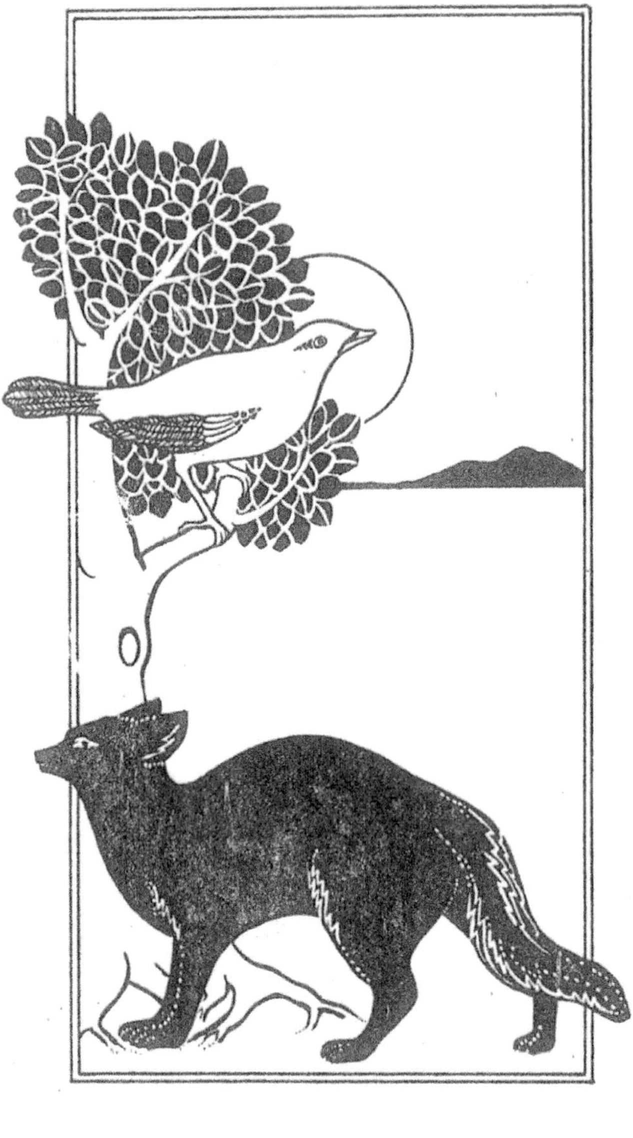

The Fourteenth Night

Now shines the silver orb of Iran's night

Clear o'er the stony hills and uplands bare,

Diminishing the fiery sun-god's might

And tempering with her gaze the enfevered air.

Now wander shades of long-departed kings,

But all in vain they seek their glorious homes,

For where their trumpets called, the nightbird sings,

And where their armies tramped, the jackal roams.

On some such night as this my memories crowd,

Of journeyings in that age-old storied land,

Of Shirin peerless, and of Chosroe proud;

On some such night as this I understand

How that calm light, which saw the world draw breath,

Shall yet be shining, when it sinks to death.

Printed in Great Britain
by Amazon